Mercy Not Sacrifice

Mercy Not Sacrifice

Lenten Daily Reflections

Mark-David Janus, CSP, PhD

Paulist Press
New York / Mahwah, NJ

Library of Congress Cataloging-in-Publication Data
Names: Janus, Mark-David, author.
Title: Mercy not sacrifice : lenten daily reflections / Mark-David Janus, CSP, PhD.
Description: New York / Mahwah, NJ : Paulist Press, [2023] | Summary: "Inspired
by the daily scripture readings, the author shares original reflections for each day
of Lent"—Provided by publisher.
Identifiers: LCCN 2022029920 (print) | LCCN 2022029921 (ebook) | ISBN
9780809156573 (paperback) | ISBN 9780809188185 (ebook)
Subjects: LCSH: Lent—Prayers and devotions.
Classification: LCC BX2170.L4 J36 2023 (print) | LCC BX2170.L4 (ebook) | DDC
242/.34—dc23/eng/20221014
LC record available at https://lccn.loc.gov/2022029920
LC ebook record available at https://lccn.loc.gov/2022029921

ISBN 978-0-8091-5657-3 (paperback)
ISBN 978-0-8091-8818-5 (e-book)

Published by Paulist Press
997 Macarthur Boulevard
Mahwah, New Jersey 07430
www.paulistpress.com

Printed and bound in the
United States of America

For Celeste, in memory of Susan, in gratitude for John
With love for Camilla, Caleb, and his John

Introduction

"It is mercy I desire, not sacrifice, the knowledge of God rather than burnt offerings" (Hos 6:6). Lent is where we come face-to-face with mercy, our need for mercy, the experience of God's generous mercy, the challenge to be merciful to others, and perhaps hardest of all, be merciful to ourselves. It is through mercy we come to the knowledge of God.

The scripture has pride of place in guiding the Lenten journey. This book is the result of my personal reading of the scriptures assigned to each day in Lent. Lenten Sunday readings rotate on a three-year cycle, with the weekday readings being the same every year. Together they form a bedrock for Lenten reflection. During my practice of *lectio divina*[1] in Lent, on any given day one paragraph, one sentence or phrase, maybe one word jumps out and seizes my attention. What follows is neither an exegesis nor a homily on all the scriptures for that day, but simply my soul's reaction to particular words of a particular scripture.

Most of these reflections concern the Hebrew Scriptures for two reasons.

---

1. *Lectio divina* is an ancient form of prayerfully reading the Bible. For more information on this prayer form practice, I recommend: *Too Deep for Words: Rediscovering Lectio Divina* by Thelma Hall (1988/2002); *Lectio Divina: Contemplative Awakening and Awareness* by Lucy Wynkoop (2008); and *The Bible as Prayer: Handbook for Lectio Divina* by Stephen Hough (2007). If you want to try *lectio divina* for yourself, I encourage you to consult *The Catholic Prayer Bible: Lectio Divina Edition* (2010). All titles published by Paulist Press.

First, these are the scriptures Jesus prayed. While obviously I don't know how he prayed them, that he prayed them is important to me.

Second, we are less familiar with the scriptures Jesus read, Christians tend to focus on the New Testament. When I was a seminarian, Fr. Raymond Brown, the great New Testament scholar, offered an explanation: the New Testament was written within a short period of time, dominated by the hope of the resurrection and an immanent second coming of Christ. The message is upbeat, hopeful, by definition, the good news. The Hebrew Scriptures on the other hand, covers thousands of years of human struggle. If you want to explore the difficult parts of the human journey, which is where growth happens, the Hebrew Scriptures are a treasury of wisdom.

When you have ten uninterrupted minutes to yourself, read the scripture passage, however short, allowing a word or phrase to roll around inside your head. After you read my reflection, read the scripture again, searching for a word or phrase that connects to your life. Your personal reflections on these scriptures are going to be different from mine, which is why there is room for you to jot your own thoughts, and discover for yourself, the inspiration you can find from a few lines of scripture. Conclude with a prayer asking God to walk with you through the day, through the night, into tomorrow.

Lenten Daily Reflections

Lent

Seeds grow in two directions,
They send roots spreading deep into the earth
Supporting the life of stems and leaves
reaching upward toward the sun.
Human growth, being who we are,
Requires deep roots,
Nourishing our reach outward,
toward the sun, toward others, toward life,
toward God.
Lent is love moving in two directions—
A spreading search deep within our soul,
And a thrust outward beyond ourselves toward others.
Lent is time to dig deep and reach out.
We ought not waste the chance
To be the love we are made to be.

Amen

Ash Wednesday

Even now, says the Lord,
Return to me with your whole heart,
With fasting, weeping, mourning.
Rend your hearts, not your garments,
And return to the Lord your God,
Gracious,
Merciful,
Slow to Anger,
Rich in Kindness,
Relenting in Punishment.

Joel 2:12–23

Reflection

Ash Wednesday is not about me.
Ash Wednesday is not about my sin, my *mea culpa*.
Ash Wednesday is about God,
About who God is and how God reacts
when we sin.
Coming face-to-face with our shortcomings,
The selfishness or fear that keeps us from loving,
God reacts to us with mercy that includes
Understanding, comfort, patience, forgiveness,
And an absolute refusal to believe we don't
have any more love to give.
"I have come that you might have life
and have it to the full," Jesus says (John 10:10).
Life to the full means love to the full.

It means loving ourselves
—the parts we don't like
—the parts we would rather—but can't
Forget or forgive.
It means love of friends and neighbors.
By the way, our neighbor is anyone we meet who needs
our help—our mercy;
As well as those we never meet
Whose need we can't pretend we don't see.

Because God does not believe
We, at our worst, are who we truly are,
God's mercy picks us up,
dusts us off, dries our tears, erases our shame,
and sets us back on the road looking for more people to love.

Ash Wednesday is not about me, or you,
or about what we have done or have failed to do.
It is about believing
in the God whose name is mercy.
We wear a cross of ashes—signs of God's mercy and love
for sinners like you and me.
Wearing ashes doesn't mean we are sinners or saints
It means we believe in the mercy of God
Mercy for me,
mercy for you,
mercy for everyone.
This is the beating heart of the gospel.
This is what we believe.
This is what we live.
This is the name of our God.

Amen

Thursday after Ash Wednesday

I have set before you
Life and death
Blessings and curses,
Choose life
That you and your descendent may live.

Deuteronomy 30:18–19

Reflection

I'm Nobody! Who are you?
Are you—Nobody—too?
Then there's a pair of us![2]

Emily Dickinson

Who am I?
God wants to know.
God is not alone.
I want to know as well.
I know who other people think I should be.
I know who I always wanted to be, but
What has become of me?
Time and circumstances beyond my control changed me.
My expectations have been thwarted, moderated,
Adapted to reality—no choice really.

---

2. Emily Dickinson, "I'm Nobody! Who Are You?" in *Poems by Emily Dickinson: Second Series*, ed. T. W. Higginson and Todd Mabel Loomis Todd (Boston: Roberts Brothers, 1891).

I have made choices that have not turned out the way I thought.
I have done things I never thought I would do,
Things I never thought myself capable of doing.
Not all bad mind you, but for some, I wish I had a do over.
Opportunities have passed me by and will never come again.
No matter—says God—
No matter what has or has not happened to you,
No matter what you have suffered, or enjoyed,
The life I gave you is your own to do with as you please.
Please live it.
I mean really live it as the person you are created to be,
The person you choose to be.
Someone who embraces life, your life and other lives, with love.
Someone who enjoys and tends your planet so other people
now and yet to be, enjoy life too.

The ultimate curse is to forget to live, to forget to be you.
That curse is easier than you think; it is difficult to avoid.

Please, once more, once again, no matter what you have or
    haven't done,
choose life so you and your descendants may live.

Friday after Ash Wednesday

This is the fast I choose:
To loosen the bonds of injustice, to untie the thongs of the yoke,
To let the oppressed go free, and to break every yoke,
To share your bread with the hungry
and bring the homeless poor into your house,
When you see the naked, cover them,
and do not hide yourself from your own kin.

Isaiah 58:6–7

Reflection

One Lenten Friday I was invited by hymn singing Methodist men
To a breakfast of pancakes and bacon and eggs, biscuits, and
    sausage gravy,
With a vegetable omelet for their Catholic guest.
"Why do Catholics give up things for Lent…?"
"This Lent, I am giving up kale!" announced a playful questioner.
"God will reward you with a heaven of endless eternal acres
    of kale,"
I playfully replied.

God isn't the least bit interested in kale or sausage biscuits
    and bacon.
God is interested in what we give to those in need.
God is interested in who we set free from what holds them down.
Of all God is interested in, what I most fear is this,
"Do not hide yourself from your own kin."
The poor, naked, homeless, oppressed live at a distance.

My own kin, well, there is no getting away from them.
We don't get to choose our own kin.
We don't get to choose who belongs to us.

Human beings are biologically predisposed
To leave home and strike out on our own.
The drive for individuation, for mastery,
to make our own friends and choose our own spouse
with whom we will make even more kin; this is the rhythm of life.
It is not, however, an excuse to forever hide from our own kin,
Those to whom we belong, and those we have chosen.
I am not talking about abusive family members who do us harm.
God's issue is everybody else from whom we grow apart, from
        whom we hide.

We hide to avoid their needs.
We hide because they are annoying.
We hide to avoid our shame and their disapproval.
We hide because we are busy and cannot be bothered.
We hide because we have lives that do not include them.
Whatever the reason, it is much easier to give up kale
Than to pay attention to kin to whom we were born
Or kin we have chosen.

My greatest sins, sins that cannot now be undone,
Are those of hiding, ignoring family, replacing one friend
        with another
Delighted with the distance I created between us.
What if, when my eternity comes,
it is filled with endless eternal acres and acres of empty fields?

Lent is not about what we fast from, it is about who we include.

Saturday after Ash Wednesday

"Why do you eat with tax collectors and sinners?"
Jesus answered, "Those who are well have no need of a physician,
But those who are sick do. I have come to call not the righteous but
*   sinners to repentance."*

Luke 5:30–32

Reflection

I don't know if s/he was a cross dresser or transgender,
Either way, the clothes and makeup were shabby.
Having seen among those streaming into church,
many LGBTQ parishioners, she summoned the courage
to climb the steps to timidly ask, "Can I go in there, people
    like me?"
Not entirely sure of my reassurance, she spent Mass in the back,
weeping behind a statue of Mary,
leaving before any at the end of Mass could see.

Nothing is a bigger waste of time or sacrilege
Then arguments about who is worthy
To enter God's house and approach the risen Lord.
We do not need to defend the honor of God.
God does not need to be defended
By the likes of us.

To presume that we are in the position
To proclaim this one worthy, and that one not
Is to take upon ourselves a judgement belonging to God alone.
It is evidence of a righteous pride that makes Satan blush.

Doubtless any church is filled with sinners.
Any number of us profess beliefs that we do not fully live.
Doubters inhabit every pew.
Which is why the risen Lord eats and drinks with us in the
    first place,
For the healing and strength communion gives.

If we are unwilling to eat and drink with sinners
We are the ones who do not belong in God's house.

Nor are our doubts, sin, and selfishness excuses we can use
To not accept Jesus's invitation to table.
Take a chance, cross the threshold, and take your place
With people just like you, guests,
The risen Lord has called to communion.

First Sunday in Lent—Year A

Jesus was led by the Spirit into the wilderness to be tempted by the
devil. He fasted forty days and forty nights, and afterward he
was famished. The tempter came to him and said:
"If you are the Son of God, command these stones to become loaves
of bread.
If you are the Son of God, throw yourself down.
All these I will give you if you fall down and worship me."

Matthew 4:1–3, 6a, 8b

Reflection

"If you are who you think you are,
If you are loved as you say God loves you,
Then why are you poor, lonely, abandoned?
Why are you where no one notices you;
Where the world goes on about its business without you?
Where you are at best an annoyance to be ignored, and at worst,
a pest to be exterminated?"

The devil plays on the discrepancy between
Who Jesus knows himself to be—God's beloved,
And his experience, which shows no evidence of love at all.

"If God were God," the devil says, "You should want for nothing.
Attention would be paid to you; the power of the world belongs
     to you.
Isn't it time to put trust in God aside and take things into your
     own hands?

Be the master of your own destiny and do what has to be done.
Make stones into bread, be the center of attention, achieve and
    wield power."
The devil lives in the discrepancy
Between what we think should happen if God loves us
And life as we live it.
To account for discrepancy between expectations and reality
the devil whispers this explanation in our ear:
Either we are not loved, are not anything special,
Or that the love of God is not worth having. God is not worth
    trusting.

This was not the last time Jesus would hear this temptation:
The devil would chirp at Jesus crucified: "If you are the Son of God
come down from the cross, save yourself."
Jesus did not come down from his cross.
He did not turn stones into bread.
He did not lose faith in himself.
He did not lose faith in the disciples who betrayed him.
He did not lose faith in God.

Jesus was tempted by, but would not succumb to, evil's
    temptation.
God is love; Jesus tells us. Love is to be trusted always.
Whether in the desert or on the cross, love is to be trusted.
Trust that you are alive because you are loved.
Trust love that lives in you, among your imperfections.
Trust the love you receive from imperfect others.
Trust God's love even when hungry, lonely, and powerless.
Trust God's love in the face of death.
Trust you will be loved in the resurrection
Where you will only love—forever and ever, world without end.

First Sunday in Lent—Year B

*And the Spirit immediately drove him into the wilderness. He was
in the wilderness forty days, tempted by Satan; he was with the
wild beasts; and angels waited on him.*

Mark 1:12–13

Reflection

What in the world is the Spirit doing?
Driving God's beloved in the wilderness—
Into the teeth of wild beasts—where Satan can have at him?

When I think about it, I take comfort from the fact
That Jesus begins where I live, in a wilderness not friendly to life
Where I have to scratch and claw to survive
Where wild beasts chew the dreams and ideals of childhood.
Where life is not easy Satan is present,
A vulture feasting on the remains of my faith, hope, and love.

In this reality show—Jesus's only allies are angels.
Angels carry messages to and from God—we call them prayers.
Surrounded by our own wild beasts, struggling to survive
Sometimes all we have to eat and drink are prayers.

Prayer is when I stop my constant attention to me
And attend to God.
It is a time when we make ourselves listen to God.
God who speaks to us only of love,

Invites us to live in love, to allow ourselves to be loved
by the one who made us.

The whole world needs to hear more about love.
No one ever hears enough of how important they are,
how loved they are.
In the wilderness, we have to work very hard
to get any attention at all.

Prayer is just the opposite.
When we pray, God listens to every word.
When we pray, we have the attention of the Creator.
When we pray, God has nothing better to do than to attend to us,
To be present—to us—over and over again.

Satan is very clever.
Whenever we pray, Satan is paying close attention,
An eavesdropping malware telling me prayer is about me;
Prayer is all about what I need and what I want
and can be measured by how it makes me feel.
If I do not get what I want, if praying does not make me feel good,
there is no use in me praying at all.

But prayer is not about me, it is about God.
It is about believing that no matter where we are
And no matter how we feel
We can always place ourselves in the presence of
The God who loves us, attends to us, and promises never to leave
    us alone.
Even when we are in the wilderness
Surrounded by wild beasts, surrounded by evil itself,
We are not alone; in prayer God sends angels to fortify us.
Praying is practicing the presence of God.
Prayer is how we get out of the wilderness alive.

First Sunday in Lent—Year C

*Jesus, full of the Holy Spirit, returned from the Jordan and was
    led by the Spirit into the wilderness, where for forty days he
    was tempted by the devil.*

Luke 4:1–2

*When the devil had finished every test, he departed from him
    until an opportune time.*

Luke 4:13

Reflection

I don't know how long it took me to realize temptation
does not mean I am weak, but it was too long.
I practiced a spirituality that said if I was holy enough,
    disciplined enough
I will be free of temptation.
Not only ridiculous, it is a temptation all by itself.
If Jesus can be tempted by the devil, who am I to think
I cannot be tempted?

You are not in charge of your temptations, whatever they are.
The devil is the one doing the tempting.
If the symbol of the devil doesn't sing to you, try this out,
You don't live in a bubble separating you from evil.
Some evils are clear and obviously seen, but most are subtle.
Thomas Aquinas taught that the most common temptation
Is the good getting in the way of the better.
It is by small increments, almost imperceptible,

That we are tempted further and further away from our best self,
Further and further away from God
Until finally, I no longer know who I am, much less who God is.

We carry our shadow self, the seeds of our destruction, all
   our lives.
They await only the opportune moment to appear.
Again, it is not because we are bad.
No amount of therapy, no amount of spiritual direction
Or prayer—if we take Jesus's example,
Will insulate us from the "opportune moment"
That convinces me to choose the good over the better so many
   times,
that I find myself holding the thirty pieces of silver I exchanged
for choices, for betrayals, that made so much sense at the time.

The devil tempted Jesus from pursuing a life of love,
And when that didn't work, when Jesus was crucified,
Tempted him to believe his life and love was all a waste.

If I cannot stop temptation, then I have to expect it.
And pray for the attention and strength to resist
What will, at the time, seem so reasonable.

First Week in Lent—Monday

Just as you did it to the least of these, you did it to me.

Matthew 25:40

Reflection

Fr. Gene Meade was a courtly gentleman living in quiet
    retirement in Boston
Where I was his newly ordained noisy neighbor,
occasionally chastised for music that disturbed his slumbers.
A grandfather figure to my visiting younger adult sister
Who benefited more from his gentle listening
Than from my copious brotherly advice.
He asked after her often, remembering her in his prayers.

One day, Gene treated me to lunch at Locke Ober's,
An established Boston restaurant serving prominent male
    Bostonians
After lunch, walking uphill home, "Fadda—a quata, please,"
A beggar who recognized him pleaded.
Stopping, Gene opened his billfold slipped him paper money and
    a blessing.
Our journey was only a few steps advanced when we could hear
    the man
Loudly begging every passerby for more.
Again, Gene halted—looking me in the eye, said,
"That man did not start out like that."
Before continuing home to his nap.
Boston then, as the New York City where I live now,

has numerous homeless beggars living on the street.
It isn't the money Gene gave, money perhaps soon to be drunk
    or drugged
That I recall, it is his words:
"That man did not start out like that."
He saw a life whose hope and promise had come to nothing,
A life once loved and cherished, now cared for by no one.

"Give," Jesus says, "to all who ask." "Lend without expecting
    repayment."
I don't know what Jesus would do if he lived in New York
Where we have more homeless living on the streets than
    there were
People living in Judea in his time.
But I suspect, like Gene Meade, he would see not only beggars
But people whose lives had not started out that way,
Lives once cuddled, fed, encouraged—
Human beings whose lives crumbled,
And encourage us to find a way to give
Sustenance, shelter, hope, and dignity
without expecting repayment.
"Give" simply said
So many to give to
So hard to do.

First Week in Lent—Tuesday

When you pray, do not babble,
Like those who think they will be heard because of their many
*   words,*
Your Abba knows what you need before you ask.

Matthew 6:7

Reflection

Babble! Is that what Jesus thinks of my prayer?
Is that the thanks I get, I ask you!
I am an experienced babbler, capable of extended speech—
    the kind
Shakespeare calls, "all sounds and fury, signifying nothing."
While babbling away, I am thinking of me, not my poor listener.
Babbling away at others, I suppose I babble at God.

Prayer is not about me, not about what I say, or how I feel
    saying it.
Prayer is about the listener, the always attentive God.
I don't need words to get God's attention, I already have it.
Prayer is me paying attention to God.
Words are not necessary—use them, by all means,
if they help you stop and pay attention to the unseen God in love
    with you.
Prayer doesn't have to take a long time.
Just a few minutes in the shower as warm water soothes
    your body

turn your attention in gratitude, or need, to the God who
    made you,
That's enough.
Enough to know you are not alone, not ever.
Prayer is not divulging unknown secrets to God.
Prayer reminds us
God, who hears the cry of the poor even before a sound is made,
is at our side without our asking, loving even when we feel
    unloved.
This prayer gives us the courage to trust in life and live it.

First Week in Lent—Wednesday

All shall turn from their evil ways and from the violence that is in their hands.

Jonah 3:8b

Reflection

The violence in my hands is invisible.
That doesn't mean it is not there,
It's just more subtle.
Hands that pull a trigger,
Start a war,
Beat a family member,
Rob the elderly,
Rape the defenseless,
Defraud the helpless.
Violence in those hands is obvious, in the news.

My hands are private, their violence unseen
As they push the button sending sarcasm, gossip,
    humiliations, lies
Speeding across Twitter and TikTok.
No one sees them not write the letter—not place the call,
To ease the loneliness, reassure the love, of distant friends and
    relatives.
A suffering environment cannot easily trace its destruction
    to my fingerprints.

Hands, hidden in my pockets, defend no one
From hands delighting in overt violence.
Biblical language allows no escape, no excuse.
No matter how many times I wash my hands
of the innocent blood of the crucified,
Evil lives in my hands—
In what I have done and failed to do.

Hands are alive with power—
The potters touch that creates,
Hands made to comfort, caress,
Compose, cook, craft, clean, clothe.
Hands feed, shelter, build,
plant, defend, protect, heal.
Hands teach, write, play, applaud,
inspire, bless, and absolve.
All this lives in our hands,
Which is why the kingdom of God
Is at hand, your hands.

First Week in Lent—Thursday

Then Queen Esther, seized with deadly anxiety, fled to the Lord:
"Help me, Oh Lord, who am alone and have no help but you.
I am taking my life in my hands.
Put in my mouth persuasive words in the presence of the lion…
And save me from my fear."

Esther 14:1, 13–14, 19b

Reflection

Poof!
I pray to the god of Poof—
god who makes my troubles disappear—Poof!
God does not poof—not Queen Esther's God anyway.
It is not that God is uncaring about deadly anxiety,
And who does not have that nowadays?
Fears that haunt my nights and paralyze my days.
These fears, hers or ours, are not unreasonable.
They point to real forces—larger than we can withstand,
Circumstances beyond our control,
Evils striking with malice aforethought
Often, when least expected.

A woman in a man's world, Esther prays for courage to confront,
Prays that her words be wise, clever, persuasive
As she fights the prejudice that would tear her apart,
Prays to be saved from fears that urge silence.

Esther prays to the God of courage, skill, determination.
Esther prays to be saved from fears that urge her to do nothing.
Jesus prays to the same God, and so do we.
Who couldn't use a little more courage to face the day?
The courage to be rather than to hide?

First Week in Lent—Friday

If the wicked turn away from all the sins that they have
committed...
None of their transgressions shall be remembered.

Ezekiel 18:21a, 22a

Reflection

As hard as it is to forgive—it is harder to forget.
There is an innate self-protective mechanism,
A wariness we carry against those have hurt us:
"Fool me once shame on you, Fool me twice, shame on me."
Putting aside the difficulty of forgetting pain caused by others,
It pales in comparison to the memories our ego carefully
    preserves
When we know we have failed.
In part, because I have not lived up to my own expectations,
In part, because I know my actions hurt others—often those
    I love.
Once this shame takes root in my soul, it never leaves.
If other people knew, what I know about myself,
What I did—am capable of doing, they would hate me,
    as I hate me.
Hiding, I no longer trust myself,
no longer trust anything good others think or say of me.

Even God has trouble cracking the shell we build around
    ourselves.
Not even the cross convinces us.

Judgement day, we preach, will be an uncovering, a "perp walk
    of shame"
Through God's memory of our sins.
That God forgets the sins forgiven is beyond our comprehension.
Yet God does exactly that.
Failures, sins, wickedness, call it what you will, that is repented
Is forgotten—vanishes in forgiveness absolute.
Freeing us to embrace life anew—fresh and free.

Maybe this side of heaven we will never quite believe this,
Believe God is capable of what we are not, as we easily
Conjure distant memories of sin and the shame that lives
    in them.
Maybe Purgatory is where God finally obliviates these memories
So in heaven I can see myself as God sees me,
Remembering my sin no more
Embracing love anew, afresh, forever and ever.

First Week in Lent—Saturday

Love your enemies and pray for those who persecute you
So that you may be children of your heavenly Father
Who makes the sun rise on the evil and the good, and sends rain on
the righteous and on the unrighteous. For if you love those who
love you, what good is that, don't even pagans do the same? Be
perfect as your heavenly Father is perfect.

Matthew 5:44–36, 48

Reflection

"Goddamn them!"
Who says I don't pray for my enemies?
I pray with fervor and feeling: goddamn you!
Maybe even more than once a day I pray that prayer.

Jesus has gone off the deep end here—
Getting me to pray at all is hard enough
Asking me to pray for enemies is idealistic in the extreme.
While I am at it, why does the sun always seem to rise on them
And the rain always falls on me; how is that fair?

Jesus believes we have within us the power to love as God loves,
And from time to time, we can almost see it.
Every once in a while, someone loves us that way,
And whether they know it or not, we love someone that way.
It doesn't happen all the time.
Loving people who love us is harder than Jesus lets on.

Loving enemies, praying for enemies, is incomprehensible,
Especially since Jesus does not say they stop being our enemies.

This Lent, meet Jesus halfway—if we can't bring ourselves to
    love them,
Try praying for them, not God damn them, but God bless them.
How is that for penance?

Second Sunday in Lent—Year A

Jesus took Peter, James, and his brother John, and led them up a high mountain, by themselves. And he was transfigured before them, and his face shone like the sun, and his clothes became dazzling white....Suddenly there appeared to them Moses and Elijah, talking with him.... Suddenly, a bright cloud overshadowed them, and from the cloud a voice said, "This is my Son, the Beloved, with him I am well pleased. Listen to him!"

Matthew 17: 1–3a, 5

Reflection

For the devil to capture your soul, for evil to work its way into
>   your heart,
it must first steal your memory. Not just any memory, your
>   good memories:
memories of feeling loved, held, happy;
memories of feeling curious, encouraged, excited;
memories of belonging, friendship, safety;
memories of hope, dedication, desire.
God writes these memories into our souls.
These memories of being loved and the desire to love;
Memories of beauty and creation,
Memories of our ability to create, play, and protect.
God's love is spoken to us in these memories.
Naturally the devil wants us to forget that we were ever loved,

That we ever belonged, that we were ever brave, that we
    love to play,
Love to create, love beautiful things, love friends,
That we care for people who hurt, that we oppose evil.
Prayer is when we remember everything the devil wants us
    to forget.

Jesus climbs the mountain to pray, as he prays, he remembers
All the ways God's love has been written into his soul.
He remembers that he is God's beloved, as he remembers, he
    experiences it,
He shines, he glows, he looks different—even his friends see the
    difference.
Jesus climbs the mountain to pray because when he comes down
    the mountain everything is going to go wrong. Everything
    that can go wrong will.
When everything goes wrong it seems things will go wrong
    forever.
We forget that we were ever loved—and don't think we ever will
    be—ever again.

The devil will whisper in his ear that God no longer loves Jesus.
There is no God to love Jesus, no one loves Jesus.
Helplessness, pain, and loneliness is all there is.
What does Jesus do on the cross? What does Jesus do while he
    is dying?
He prays, he remembers, he remembers the love God writes in
    his soul,
The love that will raise Jesus from the dead.

In Lent, do what Jesus did: remember, remember all the ways
in which you have felt love, enjoyed life, relished beauty,
Healed pain, and fought evil.
Start with your earliest memories and work your way forward,

through all the people and all the experiences
that have changed you, loved you, made you shine, made you glow,
made you strong, left you trusting that God loves you.

Like Jesus, we have lots of other memories:
Suffering, loneliness, disappointment.
The devil wants you to make these memories
More important than your memories of love.
Don't let the devil do it.
Even if like Jesus, everything is going wrong,
and you are hanging on your cross
Don't let the devil make the evil that has happened in your life
Stronger than the love.
The only way to do that is to pray, pray hard, pray often.
Hold tight in prayer all your memories of love,
Knowing that the God that writes them will raise you from death
    to life.

Second Sunday in Lent—Year B

When they came to the place that God had shown him, Abraham built an altar there and laid wood. He bound his son Isaac, and laid him on the altar, on top of the wood. Then Abraham reached out his hand and took the knife to kill his son.

But the angel of the Lord called to him from heaven, and said, "Abraham, Abraham!" And he said, "Here I am." He said, "Do not lay your hand on the boy or do anything to him."

Genesis 22:9–12

Reflection

In the world in which Jesus lived, in the world in which we live,
Protecting love requires sacrifice, real sacrifice.
Not giving up things for Lent,
But giving up ourselves, sacrificing ourselves:
Our pleasure, our time, our resources,
Sacrificing getting our own way—insisting on our opinion.

In our dangerous world,
love, God's love, the love that can change us, fills us, transfigure us,
requires sacrifice.

But we do not sacrifice children.
The story of Abraham's willingness to sacrifice his son
Only to be stopped by God's angel was told to show
God did not want the practice of human sacrifice to continue.

We do not sacrifice children:
Not to school shootings,
Not to bombing in Ghouta, Syria, Ukraine.
We do not sacrifice schoolgirls in Dakar to the sexual slavery of
    Boko Haram.
We do not sacrifice children who are Black, Hispanic, Asian.
We do not sacrifice children whose crime
Is that they are like all of us—children of immigrants.
We do not sacrifice children when they tell us they are
gay or lesbian or transgender.

Abraham was lucky,
God sent an angel to wrestle the knife out of his hand
When he was to sacrifice his child.
Who will be the angel that will prevent us
From sacrificing our children to school shootings,
to sexual slavery, to bombing, to racism, to deportation,
to the expectation to be who they are not?

Who is the angel who will tell us as he told Abraham
That his ideas were wrong?
His religious and cultural practice—hateful?
Who is the angel who will tell us as he told Abraham
The sacrifice God truly desires?
We have no angel to forcibly stop us.
But we do have Jesus, filled with love, transfigured by love;
We do have Jesus to inspire us
To change the world the only way it can be changed—
By sacrificing ourselves for another.

Second Sunday in Lent—Year C

Jesus took with him Peter, and John and James, and went up on the mountain to pray. While he was praying, the appearance of his face changed, and his clothes became dazzling white. Suddenly they saw two men, Moses and Elijah standing with him....Peter and his companions had stayed awake, they saw his glory, and the two men who stood with him. Peter said to Jesus, "Master it is good for us to be here; let us make three dwellings, one for you, one for Moses, one for Elijah."

Luke 9:28b–30, 32–33

Reflection

Almost always I observe Lent as if nothing else is happening.
Lent is my prayer, my fasting, my almsgiving.
I do the same thing year after year, and there is a comfort in that.
It is my purple bubble of devotion separating me from a
    difficult world.
I am not the first to make that mistake.

Jesus climbs the mountain, and is transfigured,
His face and appearance changed like the face of everyone in
    love changes.
Reaching back to his ancestors, Moses and Elijah,
Jesus experiences God's love in a way we have never seen before.
His friends are happy for him as we are happy when those
    dear to us
Are loved in a way that makes them glow.

That love becomes for Jesus the hope
he carries down the mountain into bad times.
He carries that hope just as he carries his cross.
Hope is his last breath, the love that carries him back to God.

We are in hard times getting harder.
What we bring to conflict is hope,
Hope born of love, born of the conviction that
God loves us always no matter the suffering and power
wreaked by Satan and all his works.
We are armed with the hope that human dignity is worth
    fighting for
no matter the cost.
Like Peter, James, and John, I want to stay where times are good,
Build my tent and live where love is obvious.
Who wouldn't want to stay there?
Satan is counting on us to stay there, leaving everybody else
    to him.

Hope born of love is not just for the war-torn places of the world:
Syria, Rwanda, Myanmar, Ukraine, Lebanon.
Hope born of love is what we carry
As we carry all the crosses, all the sufferings, burdens, sacrifices
Of our lives, and they are many.
Not as many as some, but enough, more than enough to weigh
    us down.
What good is Lent when so many in the world suffer?
Lent reminds us we are loved. God's love for us gives us hope.
Hope born of love is the courage we bring to life.

Second Week in Lent—Monday

Do not judge and you will not be judged.
Do not condemn and you will not be condemned.
Forgive and you will be forgiven.
Give and it will be given to you....
The measure you give is the measure you get back.

Luke 6:37–38

Reflection

Lenten Verbs:
Be compassionate
Do not judge
Do not condemn
Pardon
Give
Christianity is simple.
It takes all our soul, all our mind, all our heart, all our strength.

Second Week in Lent—Tuesday

"Cease to do evil, learn to do good; seek justice, rescue the
  oppressed,
Defend the orphan, plead for the widow.
Come, let us reason together," says the LORD.
"Though your sins be like scarlet, they shall be white as snow;
Though they are red like crimson, they shall become like wool."

Isaiah 1:17–18

Reflection

> We cannot escape history;…we will be remembered in
> spite of ourselves….In giving freedom to the slave, we
> assure freedom to the free—honorable alike in what
> we give, and what we preserve. We shall nobly save, or
> meanly lose, the last best hope on earth. Other means
> may succeed; this could not fail. The way is plain, peace-
> ful, generous, just—a way which, if followed, the world
> will forever applaud, and God must forever bless.[3]

Abraham Lincoln sent this message to Congress
before signing the Emancipation Proclamation.
He knew what God spoke in Isaiah, we cannot undo our past.
The suffering we caused cannot be undone.
Scar tissue remains, opportunities are lost, relationships do fail.

---

3. Abraham Lincoln, Annual Message to Congress, Washington, DC, December 1, 1862, https://www.abrahamlincolnonline.org/lincoln/speeches/congress.htm.

Nevertheless, the image and likeness of God in which we are
      created
is not erased, the ability to love remains,
and the good we do changes us.
In bestowing grace, we receive it.
The image and likeness of God glistens within anew
as our lives reflect God's generosity and justice for those who
      need it most.

Second Week in Lent—Wednesday

You know the rulers of the Gentiles lord it over them, and their great ones make their authority felt. It shall not be so among you; but whoever wishes to be great among you must first be your servant, and whoever wishes to be first among you must be your slave; just as the Son of Man came not to be served but to serve, and to give his life as a ransom for many.

Matthew 20:24–27

Reflection

Her eyes were dark, worn, quiet, kind,
Peering above a blue mask
As she changed a bloodied sheet.
"Bernieeeeeeeeeece," called the nurse,
And throughout the night
Bernice, owner of those tired eyes, came.
Each time, drifting in the dark—
kindly changing the mess.
"Roll this way just a little, honey, and now this way."
In the night after surgery,
hers are the only eyes I remember.
Tired brown eyes—gently tending spoiled linen,
tucking in yet another stranger
she would never see again,
guiding me through the night.

Second Week in Lent—Thursday

More torturous than all is the human heart,
Who can understand it?
I, the LORD alone, test the mind and search the heart.

Jeremiah 17:9

Reflection

"More torturous than all is the human heart."
Boy, is that true.
Hearts have a mind of their own sometimes.
We can't figure out our own hearts—much less someone else's.
We cannot control them, we can't understand them
And by God, we can't soothe them.
We try, without success, to self-medicate the torture and
    confusion within.
"The heart wants what it wants—or else it does not care," wrote
    Emily Dickinson,[4]
But why do I want it, why can't I have it?

There is a special agony is witnessing the tortured heart of
    the young
Who have so much to live for, so much love to give, and cannot
    see it,
Love bounces off the impenetrable shell imprisoning their hearts.

---

4. From Dickinson/M. Bowles Correspondence, spring 1862 (letter 262).

Ordinary life, to say nothing of abuse, depression,
memories that will not fade, anxieties that will not relent
relationships no longer ours,
confuse, yes, even torture a human heart
so it no longer recognizes itself—or what it is doing, or why.
It sounds like wishful thinking
asserting the Lord probes the mind and tests the heart,
Peeling away its shell, calming the hurricane,
Providing space in which we choose
Who we are, what we want, what we will do.
But I tell you, I have seen it done.
All the tools at God's command: beauty, music, art, play, touch,
The voice of a friend, stranger, family member,
Professional healers, TikTok companions, a pet, a prayer.
Anything and everything on and above the earth,
God uses it all, and without taking the credit,
Hope seeps in, purpose is revealed, sleep is easy,
And joy cometh in the morning.

We may not know what is in a human heart, even our own, but
    God does.

Second Week in Lent—Friday

Now Israel loved Joseph more than any other of his chil-
dren, because he was the son of his old age; and he made
him a coat of many colors. But when his brothers saw
their father loved him more than all his brothers, they
hated him, and could not speak peaceably to him....They
sold him for twenty pieces of silver.

Genesis 37:3–4, 28b

Reflection

O beware, my lord, of jealousy;
it is the green-eyed monster which doth mock the meat it
    feeds on.

Merchant of Venice, Act 3 scene 3

Jealousy and sister envy are frequent guests in books, plays, and
    scripts because they are frequent visitors in life.
The basic human instinct for mastery, to be the best we can be,
sits on a razor's edge.
On one side is inspiration for striving, on the other is hatred.
Either hatred for those who are more skilled at this or that than I,
or self-hatred for not being as good as others.
Bullying feeds on the need to make someone less, so I can
    be seen,
or at least feel superior to someone else.
In the extreme, jealousy plays a role in centuries of racial hatreds,
and in the extreme—justifies genocide.

Focusing on who has more of something than do we, and who
    has less,
means we have been tempted away from the truth
that God made us as we are, calls us good,
good enough to be God's image and likeness.
If I cannot delight in the beauty of my soul,
if all I can do is envy or disparage the beauty of yours,
I am selling your dignity and mine for far less than twenty pieces
    of silver.
The image and likeness of God calls us to strive to be our
    best selves,
to celebrate others that do,
and encourage those who do not see their beauty and value
    to God.

Second Week in Lent—Saturday

*Who is a God like you who removes guilt and passes over
    transgressions?*
Who does not hold on to anger forever but delights in mercy?
*God will again have compassion on us…stomp our iniquities
    underfoot and cast all our sin into the depth of the sea.*

Micah 7:18–19

Reflection

Who is a God like you? Not me, that's for sure.
Guilt clings to me like my skin.
And if you think my sins are the only ones I remember,
You have another think coming.
When I think of what other people have done to me
—no matter how long ago—
Anger explodes like fireworks on the 4th of July.

Once upon a time, Saturday meant going to confession—if you
    were Catholic.
People lined the aisles until it was their turn to slip into the box
And remind God of their sins.
If it was a dull week, you could always confess past or
    forgotten sins.
In exchange, you escaped the fires of hell,
Although a lifetime of sins would have to be revisited in purgatory.

If you weren't religious at all, not to worry, Freud points out that
    past sins

Hide in one defense mechanism or another, jumping out
From time to time reminding us—we are not who we think we are.

How unlike God we are, who, according to Micah
Has a bottle of guilt remover, stomps on sin like collapsing a box,
And throws all of it into the sea of infinity—where even God can't
    find it.

Confession is not about us yelling, I did it! I did it!
As if we were on a witness stand in a courtroom drama.
Confession is about confessing our belief in God's mercy.
Acknowledging we know what we have done and have
    failed to do.
Asking God for the mercy that gives us courage to do better,
To make our best effort at healing the wounds we have caused,
and then we let it go and live our life.
Confession helps me remember it is not all about me.
Confession helps me remember an image of God I too
    easily forget.

I like Micah's active imagery: God removing guilt, stomping
    on sins,
throwing them where they will never be seen again.
If God is energetic about it,
convinced I can't really live carrying your sins and mine
    everywhere I go, maybe I should pay attention.
With all due respect to my patron saint Freud,
Stuffing them into my attic of defense mechanisms is not enough.
Maybe I should take a page out of God's book,
Stomping, treading, letting go, casting all of that away—
And with all the compassion I can muster—live my life,
A life of faith, hope, and love.

Third Sunday in Lent—Year A

So he came to a Samaritan city called Sychar, near the plot
of ground that Jacob had given to his son Joseph. Jacob's
well was there, and Jesus, tired out by his journey, was sit-
ting by the well. It was about noon. A Samaritan woman
came to draw water, and Jesus said to her, "Give me a
drink." (His disciples had gone to the city to buy food.) The
Samaritan woman said to him, "How is it that you, a Jew,
ask a drink of me, a woman of Samaria?" (Jews do not
share things in common with Samaritans.) Jesus answered
her, "If you knew the gift of God, and who it is that is say-
ing to you, 'Give me a drink,' you would have asked him,
and he would have given you living water." The woman
said to him, "Sir, you have no bucket, and the well is deep.
Where do you get that living water? Are you greater than
our ancestor Jacob, who gave us the well, and with his sons
and his flocks drank from it?" Jesus said to her, "Everyone
who drinks of this water will be thirsty again, but those
who drink of the water that I will give them will never be
thirsty. The water that I will give will become in them a
spring of water gushing up to eternal life." The woman said
to him, "Sir, give me this water, so that I may never be
thirsty or have to keep coming here to draw water."

John 4:4–15

Reflection

This side of heaven I think it is impossible for us, even for
the saints,

To realize how thirsty Jesus is for us. Thirst is more than
wanting something.
Thirst is a need, a craving, a cry for something we cannot
live without.
To want something so much, to have a desire so captivating
That it hurts not to have it. That is how thirsty Jesus is for you
and me.

If it was as simple as asking someone for a drink of water,
We all know how to do that. The woman at the well knew how to
do that.
It's more than that.

We, like the woman, are sitting on the edge of the well of our lives
Jesus is saying to us, "Give me what you have.
Open your heart. Give me who you are. Whatever you are:
Believing, disbelieving, confused, faithful, unfaithful,
Frightened or courageous, loving or fearful, weak or strong.
In the first chapters or final chapters of your life, give me a drink.
Your strength, your love, your life, you, are the well that quenches
my thirst."

To give Jesus a drink of water means opening our lives to
God's love,
God's Holy Spirit animating the best of ourselves,
And our best is when we are compassionate, forgiving,
Generously using our skills, talents, art, creativity,
Intelligence, and hard work, to quench the thirst of others.

People are dried out, dehydrated by loneliness, lack of food,
water,
Respect, laughter, human touch, attention, friendship,
and yes, all too many in this world who remain thirsty for
clean water.

When we give any of these people a drink—and they are all
      around us—
Family, friends, neighbors, strangers, close at hand and in
      faraway places.
When we give any of these a drink from the reservoir of our
      human heart,
We are breathing the Holy Spirit, doing what Jesus needs us to do,
Giving others a drink of the life that never ends, the water of
      God's love;
The water flowing from his side at the cross,
The water that dripped on us in our baptism,
The water we now give so others can live.

I cannot do that, not for long anyway,
unless I know God's thirst, God's love for me.
How can I do that, knowing what I know about me?
For my thirst is greedy, often apathetic to the thirst of others,
And, if not apathetic, overwhelmed by their thirst,
fearful their thirst will drain me.

Dare I bring me and my worst to the cross of the one who thirsts
      for me,
And leave behind, my worst?
Dare I drink of the blood and water flowing from his side?
Do I risk being refreshed by the God
who loves even the worst of me so that I love with the best of me;
able, willing, eager, to quench the thirst of anyone who asks me
      for a drink?
Dare I let the risen Lord Jesus give me the drink of living water
That quenches my thirst and changes my life?

Third Sunday in Lent—Year B

Then God spoke these words:
"I am the LORD your God, you shall have no other gods besides me.
You shall not take the name of the LORD your God in vain.
Remember to keep holy the sabbath day.
Honor your father and your mother.
You shall not kill.
You shall not commit adultery.
You shall not steal.
You shall not bear false witness against your neighbor.
You shall not covet your neighbor's house
You shall not covet your neighbor's wife or male or female slave, or
    ox or donkey, or anything that belongs to your neighbor."

Exodus 20:1–17

Reflection

There are lots of things we do not know.
But one thing we do know, and have known since the days of
    Moses,
Is how God wants us to live life.
"I am the LORD your God who brought you out of the Land of
    Egypt and
you shall have no other gods before me, you shall carve no
    idols for
yourselves and worship them."
God the creator of heaven and earth is the lord of human history,
your story and mine.
We are willed into existence to know God, love God, and serve God.

We are not alone, never have been and never will be.
Only God is worthy of our life, our labor, and our love.
To those who say that that there is no God,
that awe and beauty are transitory phenomena;
to those who make gods of their own ambitions, needs,
and longing for power, importance, and pleasure,
we say there is no God but God, and God is one,
and to go through life ignoring the one who created us in love
    and for love
is tragedy beyond words.

You shall not take the name of the Lord your God in vain.
We swear to God all the time: to love, honor and cherish our
    spouse,
forsaking all others for as long as we live.
We swear that we will raise our children to know and love God.
We swear loyalty to our friends.
We swear that we will tell the truth, so help us God.
We swear that we will carry out the duties of our public office
with honor, in truth, and without self-interest, so help us God.
We swear that we will do no harm to our patients,
That we will represent our client's best interest,
That we will be honest in business.
Priests swear obedience and respect to our bishop,
We swear we will live what we preach,
We swear that we will be as holy as the actions we perform.
When we make a promise in God's name
We should keep it. We should not take it in vain.

We must keep holy the Sabbath.
On the seventh day God rested.
So, no work may be done by you, or your son or your daughter
Or anyone who works for you, or your beasts.
When the Romans and Greeks encountered the Jewish practice

of setting aside the Sabbath for rest, prayer, and pleasure,
they voiced an opinion that is universal among capitalists of today:
that it is a lazy, outdated, economically unviable practice
to sacrifice 1/7th of all the time and energy we possess.
We are a nation of Sabbath breakers,
The Sabbath tells us that we do not live to work, we live to love.

In the remaining commandments
God calls our attention to the ways in which we live with each
     other,
starting with our family and then moving outward
into all the concentric circles of relationships.
God cannot be contained anywhere but must be loved everywhere.

Honor your father and your mother.
We begin life being honored by them, loved by them,
not for anything that we have done, or will do, but just because
     we are.
President Obama told the story of being woken up by his
mother at 4:30 in the morning so that she, a single mother,
could read to him before she had to go to work and he to school.
When he complained, she replied, "This is no party for me either."
Wisdom happens when we recognize that our parents are people
who need to be loved, too.
They need to be honored, as they have honored us with their
     sacrifice.

Thou shall not kill...period.
Catholics shall not kill Protestant or Jew;
Sunni shall not kill Shia; Tutsi shall not kill Ibo;
Jews should not kill Palestinians, or Palestinians kill Jews;
Russians should not kill Ukrainians; Hindus should not kill
     Catholics;

Catholics shouldn't kill anybody.
Thou shalt not kill in abortion clinics or on death row or in
    Guantanamo.
Thou shalt not kill African Americans, or gays, or immigrants
    from Mexico.
Thou shalt not kill the environment.
To those who argue that violence is an inevitable form
of political resolution, we repeat the words of St. Pope Paul VI:
"War never again, never again war."

Thou shalt not commit adultery.
Relationships are sacred. Sex is not forbidden but it is sacred.
Because sex is sacred, I cannot say with my body
what I do not mean in my own heart,
I do not make a commitment with my body that I will not keep in
    my heart.
Human bodies are indeed beautiful and indeed
we long to touch and be touched,
but bodies belong to human beings who are sacred to God.

To those who say that truth is a matter of perception and
    opportunity,
that facts are subject to spin, and speech is the art of persuasion,
God says, "Thou shalt not bear false witness."
St. Paul says it more brutally: "Stop lying to each other."
Our words should honestly tell the story of our life.

Do not covet: your neighbor's house, wife, male or female slave,
    nor his ox or his ass, or anything that belongs to him.
Life is not about things, and you are not the measure of what you
    possess.
Not only should you not measure yourself by the possessions of
    others,

you should not compare yourself to others.
All by yourself, naked as God made you,
you are loved beyond imagination, valued beyond
   comprehension.
Greed in all its forms is a temptation to exchange being loved for
   acceptance;
the temptation to exchange our self-worth for the worth of
   things;
the temptation to not believe that the love of God is enough;
the temptation to believe we are not enough for God.
More could be said of the Ten Commandments.
More has been said, and even more should be said.
But what cannot be said is that we do not know them.
We cannot say we do not know how God wants us to live.

Third Sunday in Lent—Year C

*God called out to him out of the bush, "Moses, Moses! Come no
    closer.
Remove the sandals from your feet, for the place on which you are
    standing is holy ground....I am God."*

Exodus 3:4–6

Reflection

Where is your holy ground?
The place where holiness rises up through your feet—
And you feel yourself in a special place, call it a holy place,
Where God speaks to you.

I started to make a list of my holy places:
The porch of the Paulist house at Lake George,
The sands of Hoffmaster State Park and Hilton Head Island,
El Capitan at Yosemite,
The reflection of Mt. Denali in Mirror Lake.
While you may laugh, the practice areas of almost any golf course.
The color of fall leaves on the soccer pitch,
The sound of hockey skates on the ice.
The heat of my grandmother's kitchen,
The coal cellar filled with the aroma of grandfather's horseradish.
A pink chair in my younger sister's living room.

There are more conventional holy sites:
St. Joseph Oratory in Montreal—where my older sister found
    blessing for polio.

The sanctuary of St. Paul the Apostle in New York:
Once holy because that's where I was ordained.
Now its holiness has nothing to do with me—
but everything to do with the faith of the people who worship
there.
Anyplace where I hear confessions, again made holy by those
seeking God.
The chapels at Mt. Savior Monastery, Spencer Abbey,
and the crypt of Edward the Confessor in Westminster.
St. Stephens Church in Mainz, where holiness glistens
through blue stained glass windows made by Chagall.
Michaelskirche in Fulda, home to Christians since the 9th
century.
The Sistine Chapel, obviously.
In St. Peter's in Rome, the first step behind the high altar
From which only Popes ascend to the Bernini altar.
Look straight up from this spot and you see right through
the center of Michelangelo's Dome into heaven.
The Church of San Clementi, a crypt beneath the city
Where persecuted Christians have prayed since the 4th century.
The reflecting pool at Platz der Alten Synagogue in Freiburg,
built in the outline of a synagogue burned during the
Kristallnacht.

My feet have stood on other holy ground, too personal to write
of here,
But I am sure you too have stood on private holy ground.
You have your own list of places you have stood,
Places made holy by their beauty,
Holy because of those who stood there before you,
Holy because of those who have stood there with you.

On this holy ground, God spoke to you.
As with Moses, you may not have known it was God speaking.

That realization may have taken time.
But from that spot, God reaches out to you.
It could be anywhere—because God is everywhere.
Make your list of holy ground.
If you do nothing else this Lent
Realize all the ground you walk on can be holy ground
through which God calls your name.
When that happens, take off your shoes and listen, stay a while
    and rest there.

Third Week in Lent—Monday

"Go wash in the Jordan seven times, and your flesh shall be restored, and you shall be clean." So Naaman became angry and went away, saying, "I thought that for me he would surely come out and stand and call on the name of the LORD his God, and would wave his hand over the spot, and cure the leprosy! Are not Abana and Pharpar, the rivers of Damascus, better than all the waters of Israel? Could I not wash in them and be clean?" He turned and went away in a rage. But his servants approached and said to him, "If the prophet had commanded you to do something difficult, would you not have done it? How much more when all he said was, 'Wash and be clean.'"

2 Kings 5:10–14

Reflection

There are times we believe more in miracles than in God.
God needs to supply special effects for us to believe.
Miracles have to dazzle or they are not miracles.
God making the world in six days, that's a miracle.
God using the Big Bang and evolution as the tool of creation,
That's not miracle enough to impress us.
Healing on demand, healing we can't explain—that's God.
The human brain that discovers penicillin, vaccine, transfusions, surgery,
Therapies that relieve trauma, that's not God.
Thunder, lightning, burning bushes, famines, plagues, earthquakes,

This is how God must get our attention.
Forest fires, famines, melting glacier continents, hurricanes, heat waves
Can't possibly be God informing us that a carefully constructed creation
Is being sinned against.
Speaking in tongues is a sign of God;
that a child learns to speak at all is nothing special.
Truths prewrapped in stone tablets from Sinai, we believe.

Centuries of accumulating knowledge,
discarding one hypothesis for another to better explain experience,
a curiosity with enough humility to continue searching
because we don't know all the truths of creation,
that's relativism, not revelation.
"If you are the Christ, come down from the cross then we'll believe" (Matt 17:40).
Compassion suffering our worst, so we believe God's best,
We can't see our way clear to believe that, even when hanging in front of us.

Cut Naaman the Syrian some slack, we, too, long for
God to perform for us the difficult, spectacular, unexplainable.
In doing so, we miss the miraculous surrounding us,
The miracle we already are.
The miraculous in which we live and move and breathe and have our being.
Try that for Lent.

Third Week in Lent—Tuesday

Then his lord summoned him and said, "You wicked slave! I forgave you all that debt because you pleaded with me. Should you not have had mercy on your fellow slave as I had with you?" And in anger his lord handed him over to be tortured until he would pay his entire debt. So my heavenly Father will also do to every one of you if you do not forgive your brother or sister from your heart.

Matthew 18:32–33

Reflection

I want to look at this from a slightly different slant.[5]
Forgiveness is more than avoiding threats of divine torture.
Jesus asks us to be perfect as the heavenly Father is perfect
   (Matt 5:48),
To love, as God loves.
Whatever you and I think about God, it's not enough.
God is beyond any of our doctrinal definitions,
And is not limited to any parentheses of action we construct.
We only know God by experience. Athanasius the Great wrote,
"God became a human being, so human beings might
   become God."[6]
This doesn't mean we join the Trinity or populate heaven like
   Greek gods.

---

5. I am indebted to Jose Tolentino Cardinal Mendonca for this insight. You can read more in his book *Our Father Who Art on Earth: The Lord's Prayer for Believers and Unbelievers* (Mahwah, NJ: Paulist Press, 2013).

6. Athanasius, *On the Incarnation* 54:3, written circa AD 335.

It means communion, union with God. We are made for that.
We do that by doing what God does, and forgiveness is what
    God does.
Mercy is who God is.
Being merciful is the path to union with God.
When we are being merciful, we are experiencing God.
True, we might not think that at the time.
Being merciful is difficult, often painful, the feeling—
    underwhelming.
We are hoping that the experience of God
Is more like Christmas than Calvary,
Comfort and joy, glory to God in the highest and all that.
Otherwise, what is the point?
The point is, the more mercy we practice,
The more we forgive our brother and sister from our hearts—
Risking the crucifixion of forgiveness—
The more we experience who and what God is.
There is no love without mercy, and Love is who we are made for.

Third Week in Lent—Wednesday

Take care and watch yourselves closely, so as neither to forget the things that your eyes have seen, nor let them slip from your mind all the days of your life, make them known to your children and your children's children.

Deuteronomy 4:9

Reflection

Kindness is slippery.
In the heat of the moment,
Under pressure, hassled, worried, worn out,
Kindness slips away,
And we don't even know it's gone.

During a particularly righteous phase of my college life
When causes were more important than people,
My zeal intertwined with my arrogance.
An upperclassman (with whom I was not close)
Stuck his red, bushy bearded head in my doorway, softly singing
The song "Easy To Be Hard" from the hot new musical *Hair*:
"Easy to be hard
Easy to be cold…
Easy to be proud
Easy to say no
Especially people who care about strangers

Who care about evil and social injustice…
How about I need a friend"[7]
And then, left—
Left me to puzzle out I was being a jerk.
Obvious to strangers, but not obvious to me.
I had no idea what he was singing about, it took me time—
more time than it should have
to realize fervor replaced friendships.
Easily, I slipped away into hard, cold, proud, heartless ambition.

The voice of that visiting red-headed angel lives in my memory.
Believe you me, kindness is slippery.
Take care and watch yourself closely;
You can slip away from being the person you want to be
More easily than you think—even when pursuing good.

---

7. "Easy to Be Hard" from *Hair*, lyrics by Gerome Ragni, James Rado, music by Galt MacDermot. Lyrics © Sony/ATV Music Publishing LLC, 1969.

Third Week in Lent—Thursday

They did not obey me or incline their ear, but in the stubbornness
Of their evil will, they looked backward rather than forward....
They stiffened their necks. They did worse than their ancestors did.

Jeremiah 7:24, 26

Reflection

The longer I live, the more backward there is to look at.
All the stuff that happened way back then,
That was a lot of work—while I am not proud of all of it,
it was the best I could do. It's what I know.
I enjoy looking backward.
Forward—seems extra work.
I don't have the energy, and maybe, not the time.

To believe in God is to look forward—always forward.
What is behind us holds the treasury that pays our way forward.
The Church is not a museum of memories, Pope Francis says,
But a source of inspiration giving us the courage to live life
    forward.

The spiritual life is always about the future,
The journey from this side of heaven to the next
Where future is all there is.

Third Week in Lent—Friday

Jesus answered, "The first is, 'Hear Oh Israel: The Lord our God,
The Lord is one; you shall love the Lord your God with all your
heart, and with all your soul, and with all your mind, and with all
your strength.' The second is this: 'You shall love your neighbor as
yourself.' There is no commandment greater than these."

Mark 12:29–31

Reflection

The word *all* is the problem.
Love is not part of our life; it is everything.
It is for everyone, not just for those with whom we are "in love."
Even they present challenges.
Loving parents, children, brothers, sisters, families, and friends
is not so easy.

Try loving on the bus or subway, stuck in traffic,
stuck in a job you hate, or can't find a job at all, try that.
Love when betrayed by the people you love.
Try that.

Try loving in the world of politics where we bump up against
    one another
Armed as we are, with conflicting ideas, priorities.

People we know are hard enough; try loving strangers.
Bullying different looking, sounding, living people begins early.

While you are trying to love imperfect people, try loving yourself.
Try loving yourself when you are unloved.
When you see imperfections, haunted by your failures,
unable to achieve your dreams,
addicted to any of the multiple things used to escape shame.
Try it when you are sick or cranky, in pain.
Try when your body does not do what you want and never
     will again.
Try loving yourself then.

In any religion of love, and there are many,
the word *all* is the problem with love.
"All" has no footnotes, escape clauses, or exemptions.
"All" persists, despite moods, conflicts, and seasons:
for richer or poorer, in sickness and in health.
"All" lasts until death does us part, and even that might not be the
     end of "all."
It is not hard for us to claim, love is love is love.
We are just not very good at it, not as good as we could be.
Not yet.

No matter who you are, what you believe—or don't,
Whether you are religious or not,
Your spiritual life is the journey to "all."

As long as we keep trying.
As long as we don't dilute "all."
As long as we keep reaching for our best,
the "all" Jesus knows is inside of us,
As long as we do that,
we are on the road to the kingdom of God
Where love is all there is,
And all we are.

Third Week in Lent—Saturday

The Pharisee prayed thus:
"God, I thank you that I am not like other people:
Thieves, rogues, adulterers, or even like this tax collector.
I fast twice a week; I give a tenth of all my income."
The tax collector, standing far off, would not even look up to
*   heaven,*
But was beating his breast saying,
"God, be merciful to me, a sinner."
I tell you this man went home justified
Rather than the other.

Luke 18:11–13

Reflection

We all have a hidden inner Pharisee,
Trumpeting, "I am better than you."
Some people are just better, holier, than others.
It's obvious, to me anyway.

If you are a religious person, your inner Pharisee will never
    understand why
Jesus always identifies with sinners—even if they keep on sinning.
You work hard to follow in Jesus's footsteps,
While some don't try very hard at all.
They do not deserve communion with the risen Lord,
While you appreciate the honor and grace having sacrificed to
    be worthy
Of his presence.

If you are, like the tax collector,
Someone whose life is checkered with mistakes,
Who can't seem to do any better,
Who lives on the wrong side of the communion rail,
You can't understand why Jesus is on your side either.
You are just glad he is, and although you don't show it
You know mercy is the only thing keeping you alive.

Fourth Sunday in Lent—Year A

"Surely the LORD's anointed is now before Samuel." But the LORD said to Samuel, "Do not look on his appearance or on the height of his stature, because I have rejected him; for the LORD does not see as mortals see; they look on the outward appearance, but the LORD looks on the heart." Then Jesse called Abinadab and made him pass before Samuel. He said, "Neither has the Lord chosen this one." Then Jesse made Shammah pass by. And he said, "Neither has the LORD chosen this one." Jesse made seven of his sons pass before Samuel, and Samuel said to Jesse, "The LORD has not chosen any of these." Samuel said to Jesse, "Are all your sons here?" And he said, "There remains yet the youngest, but he is keeping the sheep." And Samuel said to Jesse, "Send and bring him; for we will not sit down until he comes here." He sent and brought him in. Now he was ruddy, and had beautiful eyes, and was handsome. The LORD said, "Rise and anoint him; for this is the one." Then Samuel took the horn of oil and anointed him in the presence of his brothers; and the spirit of the LORD came mightily upon David from that day forward.

1 Samuel 16:7, 10–13

Reflection

God is a strange talent scout, for whom the only analytic that
    matters is the heart.
Experience, knowledge, strength—even ostensible holiness—
Overlooked—in favor of heart and soul.
David's heart was young, impulsive, naïve, untested, hungry for
    approval.
He confronted Goliath with a confidence that comes

from never having seen the wreckage of a battlefield.
His heart was gentle, sensual, lustful, took multiple wives, and
Bathsheba who was not his wife, and a historic love for Jonathan.
He played instruments, sang, and wrote songs,
danced naked in abandon joy before God.
David's heart schemed with the best of them, was ruthless
    in battle,
yet naively overlooked the treachery of his son, Absalom.
He sinned and repented in excess, did King David's heart.

If God chose such a complex heart, why not ours?
Certainly, there are points of intersection—somewhere,
Between David's heart and our own?
God's eyesight seems to peer between failures of the human heart,
And finds enough there to pick the whole package,
Nursing what is needed and sorting through the rest later.

There is no escaping that the Lord who does not see as
    mortals see
Has picked you, with your complicated heart.
Each life is a mission, each life a word God speaks to the world.
The difference between David and you is
David had no idea where his mission would lead, you do.
You are writing with your life, in your time and circumstances,
A little gospel—announcing love even as you climb your Calvary,
Announcing love to an audience skeptical of resurrected life.
The mission that is your life, the word you speak, the gospel
    you write,
You work out with God. That is your Lent.

Fourth Sunday in Lent—Year B

But God who is rich in mercy, out of the great love with which he loved us even when we were dead through our trespasses, made us alive together with Christ—by grace you have been saved and raised up with him in heavenly places in Christ Jesus, so that in the ages to come he might show the immeasurable riches of his grace in kindness toward us in Christ Jesus. For by grace you have been saved through faith and this is not your own doing; it is the gift of God—not the result of works, so no one may boast. For we are what he has made us, created in Christ Jesus for good works, which God prepared beforehand to be our way of life.

Ephesians 2:4–10

Reflection

Loathing, I loathe so called "treatment programs"
Designed to "break people down" so they can "build them"
    back up.
I have seen the results in the hollow, hopeless eyes of teenagers
    broken
through a rejection that lives now as if a cancer in their bones
stealing sparkle from their life.
Failed expectations, the imposition of shame, isolation,
Regret—greeting them first thing in the morning,
Regret—their last thought at night.

Putting the psychological malpractice aside,
Jesus never broke someone down to build them up,
Never induced guilt and self-loathing in someone
as the price to be paid for God's grace.
Mercy, great love, kindness, these are life-giving graces
Jesus is the first to give any soul wounded
By the self-doubt and self-hatred created by shame.
Salvation is an old-fashioned word—but it means this:
"For we are what he has made us, created in Christ Jesus for
    good works."
Why is that so hard to accept, in ourselves, in others?
What demonic whisper lures us away from:
"the great love that made us alive together with Christ."

Failure is the 21st-century stone thrown at any who "do not
    measure up."
Social media—the perfect tool for sneering, shaming,
    humiliating.
Why is criticism, condemnation, political hate speech, guns,
    bullets, war
more attractive than:
"the immeasurable riches of his grace in kindness toward us in
    Christ Jesus."

I confess, I do not know.
The psychologist in me doesn't know.
The priest in me doesn't know. But the priest in me knows this:
"by grace you have been saved through faith and this is not your
    own doing;
it is the gift of God—not the result of works."
The faith Paul talks about is not our faith,
It is the faith Jesus the Christ has in us, the faith Jesus the Christ
    has in God.

Here comes the theology: because of his faith, the faith of
    Jesus Christ—
There is nothing you can do that will make God love you less.
There is nothing you can do to make God love you more.
You are as God made you—created for a life of good works.
If you get that, if you believe that, if you live that for yourself
    and others
you know what salvation means.

Fourth Sunday in Lent—Year C

Now his elder son was in the field; and when he came and approached the house, he heard music and dancing. He called one of the slaves and asked what was going on. He replied, "You brother has come, and your father has killed the fatted calf, because he has him back safe and sound." Then he became angry and refused to go in. His father came out and began to plead with him. But he answered his father, "Listen! For all these years I have been working like a slave for you, and I never disobeyed your command; yet you have never given me even a young goat so I might celebrate with my friends. But when this son of yours came back, who devoured your property with prostitutes, you killed the fatted calf for him!" Then the father said to him, "Son you are always with me, and all that is mine is yours. But we had to celebrate and rejoice, because this brother of yours was dead and has come to life; he was lost and has been found."

Luke 15:25–32

Reflection

He wants them both, though only God knows why.
The younger—selfish, sensuous, scheming.
The older, selfish in his self-righteous way, happier with
    junior gone,
Not willing to spill one drop of compassion.
Me, I would dump the pair.

Doesn't the old man have any daughters—he'd be better off
    with them.

Yet, the father wants them both.
He chases after the first and tries to reason with the second.
The old man's heart wants those kids.
While I never thought of it before, isn't that what Jesus does?
Chasing after egregious sinners while trying at the same time
to convince Pharisees that mercy is what is important?
God's heart wants us and will not stop until we belong to God,
Until we are the very goodness of God.
This story, an illustration of how deeply God wants us.
The death of Jesus is the story lived out.

How to understand this God?
In the late Catholic playwright, Terrance McNally's play,
Love! Valor! Compassion! a young, gay, blind character named
    Bobby,
Speaks this soliloquy to the audience:
"Do you believe in God? […] Do you?
I think we all believe in God in our own way. Or want to.
Or need to.
Only so many of us are afraid to.
Unconditional love is pretty terrifying.
We don't think we deserve it.
It's human nature to run. But He always finds us.
He never gives up.
I used to think that's what other people were for,
Lovers, friends, family. I had it all wrong.
Other people are as imperfect and as frightened as we are.
We love, but not unconditionally.
Only God is unconditional love,
And we don't even have to love Him back.

He's very big about it.
I have a lot of reservations about God.
What intelligent, caring person doesn't lately? [...]
But the way I see it,
He doesn't have any reservations about me.
It's very one-sided. It's unconditional.
Besides, He's God. I am not."[8]

Whether you believe in God or not, no matter what happened in
      the past
or you believe about the future, now is time only for love.
God will keep trying to convince you
To love, to forgive, to celebrate, to draw others
into the web of God's unconditional love.
That is the way God is and God is not going to give up
Until God gets you.

---

8.   Terrance McNally, *Love! Valor! Compassion!* (New York: Dramatists Play Services), 63.
Used with permission.

Fourth Week in Lent—Monday

I am about to create new heavens and a new earth;
The former things shall not be remembered or come to mind.
Be glad and rejoice forever in what I am creating.

Isaiah 65:17–18a

Reflection

Every day
We open our eyes to a new heaven and new earth.
There are days we don't feel that.
Days that feel like one damn thing after another, only
I am more tired today than yesterday,
With no solutions to the same problems.
There is only the same old me, dreading getting out of bed,
Drudging along.

God has taken the job of reminding us it doesn't have to be
    that way.
We don't have to be that way.
God creates each day alive with possibilities—our possibilities.
Daily, we are recreated—fresh hope—new eyes—new desire.
We are the new God brings to the same old same old.
We have a role to play in God's ongoing creation,
One day at a time, One dream at a time,
One foot in front of the other.

Fourth Week in Lent—Tuesday

Now in Jerusalem there is a pool called Beth-zatha, with five porticoes.

> *In these lay many invalids—blind, lame, and paralyzed. One man was there who had been ill for thirty-eight years. When Jesus saw him lying there and knew he had been there a long time, he said to him, "Do you want to be made well?" The sick man answered him, "Sir, I have no one to put me into the pool while the water is stirred up, someone else steps down ahead of me." Jesus said to him, "Stand up, take up your mat and walk." At once the man was made well, and he took up his mat and began to walk.*

John 5:2–9

Reflection

When his patients could not imagine life without suffering,
A life where they could be and do what they wanted,
Sigmund Freud wrote that the patient had to, for a limited time,
Borrow the ego of the therapist
Until they were strong enough to go it on their own.

That phrase rings true to me.
As a psychologist there are times when I have had to assure people
That, even though they don't think they can be better,
I know they can.
I am not asking them to believe what they feel,

I am asking them to believe me.
I know they can heal, be free, be who they want to be.
The work of therapy is hard and long,
and unless they believe that I believe,
unless they trust me—they will quit on themselves.
They have to "borrow my ego" until they experience a strength
they don't know they have.
All of us get stuck and need someone who believes in us more
than we do,
Who looks through our discouragement to see in us what
we don't.
We are the paralyzed person who cannot make it into the waters
of life—
Someone is always cutting ahead, reaching the life we want
before we can get there, leaving us behind.

When that person comes into our lives, we do well to
believe them
more than we believe the experience of our own pain,
more than our memory of trying again and again, only to fail.
When they tell us we can stand up, and go home to a new life,
We have to believe them—more than we believe ourselves
Or we will never move.
That sort of trust, trusting another despite our experience, that's
what faith is.

We both give and receive faith.
Sometimes I am the paralyzed who needs to believe what I
don't feel.
Sometimes I am the person believing in someone who lost faith
in themselves.
Sometimes I have to trust another.
Sometimes they have to trust me.
That's how we get through life.

Jesus is the person we believe about the God of love.
We trust the God Jesus sees in us when we don't feel anything.
That's what faith is, and is the only way we will stand up, pick up
our mat
And go home, walking under our own power, into the rest of
our lives
this side of heaven and beyond.

Fourth Week in Lent—Wednesday

Can a woman forget her nursing child, or show no compassion for the child of her womb? Even these may forget, yet I will not forget you. See, I have inscribed you on the palms of my hands.

Isaiah 49:15–16a

Reflection

Forgotten, to be forgotten, is anything worse?
To be left behind, left alone, as if not even there,
Not worth remembering, pushed into the corner, not needed.
We are a waste of space required for something useful.
To be forgotten is to be unmade, not worth time.

The ranks of the forgotten are swelling,
The health of the planet joining their number.
From time to time, and maybe for a long time,
We take our place in line with the forgotten.
The devil makes work of this dreary empty pain,
Convincing us to take the blame for the negligence of others.
We are forgotten because we are forgettable.

No, no, no, no, no, no, no!
God whispers. I don't care who has forgotten you;
I am the mother who never forgets her child.
The hungrier you are, the more you cry out,
The more I remember you, the closer you are held.
You are written on the palm of my hand.

The palm of my hand.
When you next look at a crucifix,
The nails through Jesus's palms, securing him to the cross
is how deeply you are inscribed in the hands of God.

God cannot make people pay attention to who is precious, not
even Jesus.
When you are neglected as Jesus was neglected
You are not forgotten by God any more than Jesus was forgotten.
You are held by love, in God's good, safe, strong hands.

Fourth Week in Lent—Thursday

The LORD said to Moses, "I have seen this people, how stiff necked they are. Now let me alone so my wrath may burn hot against them and I may consume them." But Moses implored the LORD, and said, "O LORD, why does your wrath burn hot against your people whom you brought out of the land of Egypt with great power and a mighty hand? Why should the Egyptians say, 'It was with evil intent that he brought them out to kill them in the mountains, and to consume them from the face of the earth?' Turn from your fierce wrath; change your mind and do not bring disaster on your people. Remember Abraham, Isaac, and Israel, your servants, how you swore to them by your own self, saying to them, 'I will multiply your descendants like the stars of heaven, and all this land I have promised I will give to your descendants, and they shall inherit it forever.'" And the LORD changed his mind about the disaster that he planned to bring on his people.

Exodus 32:9–14

Reflection

How can you not love this story, Moses talking God off the ledge?
Cooling off a divine wrath with the memory of God's past
    promises?
The world is made of stories, and this very human story
Teaches us the importance of praying for others.

I don't think we have to talk an angry God off the ledge.
Relieving the pains of others does not depend on how convincing
God finds our prayers. God intends only the good.
We are part of that good, part of an ongoing creation,
Our prayers are part of the evolutionary process.
Jesus prayed, interceding for others, why not do the same?

Midway through Lent it wouldn't be a bad idea.
Pick one person a day and open our heart in prayer for them.

Fourth Week in Lent—Friday

Let us lie in wait for the righteous man because he is inconvenient to us and opposes our action; he reproaches us for sins against the law, accuses us of sins against our training, calls himself a child of the Lord. The very sight of him is a burden to us, his manner of life is unlike that of others and his ways are strange....Let us see if his words are true, and test what will happen at the end of his life. Let us test him with insult and torture, so we may find out how gentle he is and make trial of his forbearance. Let us condemn him to a shameful death, for according to what he says, he will be protected.

Wisdom 2:12–15, 17, 19–20

Reflection

There is a special courage needed
To be who you are.
There is a special injustice reserved just for you,
Wielded by those who find you inconvenient,
Your manner of life unlike that of others, your ways strange.
There are those who resent it when, being as you are,
You claim to be a child of God.
Insult, torture, persecution will follow you, they will not rest
Until they shame the gentleness out of you.

Not only individual souls, entire groups of people, are objects of
reproach.

One ethnic group after another, each shade of color,
people of different worship, women, LGBTQ,
even children in school with a manner of life unlike others
are picked out for testing with insult, as was Jesus.

The special courage needed to be who you are—is found in your
     gentleness.
Gentleness is a strength beyond your enemies' comprehension.
Gentleness lies at the core of your soul.
Jesus taught a prayer to protect your gentleness when attacked,
     pray it often:
"Lead us not into temptation and deliver us from evil."

Fourth Week in Lent—Saturday

O LORD my God, in you I take refuge; save me from all my pursuers
And deliver me, or like a lion they will tear me apart.

Psalm 7:1–2a

Reflection

When there is no place else—that's what God is for.
Don't hesitate, there is no shame in praying for yourself.
My particular pursuer is within; cancer—the lion tearing me
    apart.
When lying inside of some medical machine,
MRI, PET scan, CAT scan, bone scan, density scan,
Injecting with fluids and swallowing pills,
There is no avoiding the fact that the lion is loose inside.
So, I pray, "Hail Mary full of Grace…pray for us sinners,
Now and at the hour of our death."
Over and over the same prayer…
Partly to distract my attention, partly to relieve my anxiety,
Partly because there is nothing else to do.
Finally, because there is no other place for me to go.
Mary full of grace doesn't begrudge me using her as a refuge.

People have told me they don't feel right praying when in trouble
because they never pray in good times.
Phooey—that is what God is for, God remembers who you are,
and is your refuge now and at the hour of your death.

Fifth Sunday in Lent—Year A

When Mary came where Jesus was and saw him, she knelt at his feet, and said to him, "Lord if you had been here my brother would not have died." When Jesus saw her weeping and the Jews who came with her also weeping, he was greatly disturbed in spirit and deeply moved. He said, "Where have you laid him?" They said to him, "Lord, come and see." Jesus began to weep. So, they said, "See how he loved him!" But some of them said, "Could not he who opened the eyes of the blind man have kept this man from dying?" Then Jesus, again greatly disturbed, came to the tomb, and a stone was lying against it. Jesus said, "Take away the stone." Martha, the sister of the dead man, said to him, "Lord, already there is a stench because he has been dead four days." Jesus said to her, "Did I not tell you that if you believed, you would see the glory of God?"

So, they took away the stone. And Jesus looked upward and said, "Father, I thank you for having heard me. I know you always hear me...."

When he said this, he cried out with a loud voice, "Lazarus come out!" The dead man came out, his hands and feet bound with strips of cloth, and his face wrapped with a cloth. Jesus said to them, "Unbind him, and let him go."

John 11:32–44

Reflection

We do not love death.
Why God created a world where death is an integral part,
We do not know—and we resent it.
If "Thou shalt not kill" is a commandment, why does God get
 to kill?
Why believe in a God who sits impassively while death claims
 every life?

When my heart is broken with death of my beloved, this becomes
 personal—
And God has something to answer for.
Why make me in the first place?
Why let me love life, if death is going to take it—take me—away?
It is pointless. It is outright cruel.

Jesus wept because the death of Lazarus hurt.
It hurt him, it hurt his friends Mary and Martha.
Jesus wept—so there are times when even God cries
 over death.
Bitterly, maybe even blasphemously, part of me is glad,
Glad God knows how it feels—knows the pain death leaves
 in its wake:
The mourning, the grieving, the endless nights and
 meaningless days,
The heart that cannot be consoled with platitudes,
The life that goes on without color or taste or music.

Jesus cries tears, the universal human language,
The only language we can speak when love has nowhere to go.
Tears come easily to some of us, others less so.
But they are there all the same—locked inside the ache where no
 words live.

Jesus wept—tears—his prayer—asking God:
"Raise Lazarus" as a sign to grieving friends that death is not all
     there is.
Jesus knows that when he dies, and he intuits it will not be
     long now—
Tears will break their heart and their faith.
They need something to hold to besides tears,
Something more than tears to believe
In his Resurrection—and the everlasting life to which it points,
not that they would understand it.
When push comes to shove, I would settle for raising the people
I love from the dead—I want them back—here and now—
Let forever take care of itself…but that misses the point.
Jesus was not raised like Lazarus.
Jesus was raised in a new body, to an everlasting life,
No more tears, death, mourning, or pain.[9]
That is what waits for us beyond death's horizon.
Love is not over when we die, nor is life.
Tears are the price of love—the price of humanity.
Tears are often our only and best prayer.
They are the angels who lead our loved into Paradise,
Not into the grave.

---

9. "God himself will be with them; he will wipe every tear from their eyes. Death will be no more; mourning and crying will be no more" (Rev 21:3b–4).

Fifth Sunday in Lent—Year B

*I tell you, unless a grain of wheat falls into the earth and dies
It remains just a single grain; but if it dies, it bears much fruit.*

John 12:24

Reflection

The grain of wheat falling to earth, dying, to produce a harvest,
Is the parable Jesus used to explain why he loved the way
    he loved.
He gives all that he is, all that he has, even his life, loving as
    God loves—
So that an abundant harvest of life would spring up,
Even as a harvest of wheat springs up from a single seed.

His disciples missed his meaning at the time
And had no idea what his crucifixion was about.
After the resurrection, they got it.
They began to understand that to love as God loves
Means spending your life—giving yourself away in love in ways
    big and small.
The grain of wheat falling to earth to produce a harvest
Was how they understood their lives as Christians.
It is how we explain why we follow the Christ today.
You are a seed of love, God's seed of love, and wherever you
    plant yourself,
Wherever and however you spend yourself, love grows all
    around you.
Wherever you live, whatever you do, however you do it,

When you spend your life in love as Jesus did his, love grows up
    around you.
You are the seed of life God has scattered on the earth
Trusting, knowing, your love has the potential to feed
untold numbers of people: the ones with whom you share
    your life,
your children, family, friends, neighbors, and more;
The hungry, the naked, the thirsty, the ill, the dying,
The imprisoned, lonely and unloved, those victimized by
    prejudice,
Misunderstood by ignorance, bullied by hate, abandoned by
    indifference.
Your life makes life happen.

God made you seeds of comfort, of beauty, of art, of taste and
    celebration
As well as the seeds of justice, equality, and solidarity.
All of that grows around you when you love as Jesus,
giving yourself away in love for those you love and for the
    unloved.
When your life is spent,
when you have given away all that you have and are,
When you surrender your last minute,
The only thing you will bring to heaven is the love you have given
    away, and,
The love you have made possible in others.

Fifth Sunday in Lent—Year C

The scribes and the Pharisees brought a woman who had been caught in adultery; and making her stand before all of them, they said to him, "Teacher, this woman was caught in the very act of committing adultery. Now in the law Moses commanded us to stone such women. Now what do you say?" They said this to test him, so that they might have some charge to bring against him. Jesus bent down and wrote with his finger on the ground. When they kept on questioning him, he straightened up and said to them, "Let anyone among you who is without sin be the first to throw a stone at her." And once again he bent down and wrote on the ground. When they heard it, they went away, one by one, beginning with the elders; and Jesus was left alone with the woman standing before him. Jesus straightened up and said to her, "Woman, where are they? Has no one condemned you?" She said, "No one, sir." And Jesus said, "Neither do I condemn you. Go your way, and from now on do not sin again."

John 8:3–11

Reflection

"They were caught in the act of adultery."
Simple words for a complex thing. How did it start?
Did they know each other for a long time, or did they just meet?
Who were they to one another? Were they neighbors?
Was he her husband's friend?
Did she babysit his children—is that how it started?

Why did they do it? Was it a fling? Did lightning strike?
Were they obsessed—infatuated? Were they unhappy in
    marriage…
they married young in those days.
Maybe their marriages didn't work—maybe they never had.
Maybe this was the first time they felt love in the longest time.
Maybe they had just grown bored with their partners;
maybe they wanted to try something new?
Who made the first move? How did they arrange to meet, at
    whose house?
Where were the children? How long had it gone on?

"They were caught in the act of adultery."
They were caught in the act.
One moment they were—whispering, touching—
then the curtains are thrown back, strangers grab and grope
and are pleased that they found what they had expected to find.
She is pulled from the bed and carried aloft like a trophy
grasping for the covers she laid under.

Did he fight for her, do you think? Did he try to protect her?
Where was he now? Did he just abandon her?
We men, we can do that. Was he even in the crowd?
Was he prepared to throw stones at her to purge his guilt?

What about the other ones?
What about her husband, his wife? How did they find out?
Are they the ones who discovered them, "in the act"
or did they hear from others?
Did they ever see each other again? Husband and wife, I mean,
    either set?
What did they say? Did they ever again touch?
How long was it till they trusted each other, or anyone ever again?

"They caught her in the act of adultery."
And used her as exhibit "A," a sinner!
That is all we are told, that's all Jesus knew.
A frightened girl, her hair askew, trembling, eyes full of tears,
her hands gathering torn sheets around her body.
She was all alone. She was guilty.
What did they want him to say?
He says nothing, Jesus does.
He doodles in the dirt, distracted, composing himself maybe,
Trying not to show his anger, who knows?
What we know is that he doodles till he stands:
"You without sin cast the first stone."
The only sinless one in the crowd says,
"You without sin cast the first stone."
You, any one of you who has never made a mistake,
any one of you who has never needed another chance,
any one of you who has never failed,
never disappointed one whom you love,
anyone who has never gone searching for love
in the wrong place, at the wrong time, with the wrong person,
you go first!
One by one they drifted away, from eldest to youngest.
those whose memories were heaviest with their own sins
went first.

When you live a long time, you know from personal experience
how many chances a human being needs.
All we know for sure is that they left,
left Jesus and the woman, "caught in the act of adultery"—alone.

"Woman, where did they all disappear to? Has no one
    condemned you?"
"They are gone my Lord?"

"Then neither do I condemn you, go now, sin no more,"
is all Jesus says.

Christians should be famous for forgiveness.
So well practiced in being forgiven, we know how to forgive
    others.
We should know how much mercy is needed.
We should know the relief that only mercy can bring.
Mercy is the greatest form of love because mercy costs us.
It is a gift that we give to someone who has hurt us, betrayed us.
It is greatest form of love because the only requirement
is that someone needs it.
It is the greatest form of love because we know this is a gift
we are asked to give again and again and again,
to the same person, to many people.
God's gift of mercy is infinite and that is a good thing
because we have infinite need of it.
We need only decide what shall fall from our hands,
stones of judgment, or the mercy of God.

Fifth Week in Lent—Monday

Then Susannah cried out with a loud voice, and said, "O eternal God, you know what is secret and are aware of all things before they come to be; you know these men have given false evidence against me. And now I am to die, though I have done none of the wicked things that they have charged against me."

The Lord heard her cry. Just as she was being led off to execution, God stirred up the holy spirit of a young lad named Daniel, and he shouted with a loud voice, "I want no part is shedding this woman's blood."

Daniel 13:42–46

Reflection

A young lad named Daniel—
The holy spirit of a young lad named Daniel—
A lad, who would have no part in the shedding of innocent
    blood—
Is how God answered Susannah's prayer,
Susannah, the victim of wicked men.

We do not have to look to see the shedding of innocent blood.
Evil men work suffering, injustice, evil, the world over.
The planet itself suffers.

Something happens to us as we age,
Something happens, some "Pilate gene" is released in us—

Innocent blood is something we wash our hands of,
Not shout out against.
We, no less than Daniel, are God's tools to answer prayers.
When God stirs our holy spirit
Whose innocent blood do we rise to defend?

Fifth Week in Lent—Tuesday

*From Mount Hor they set out by the way to the Red Sea,
to go around the land of Edom; but the people became
impatient on the way. The people spoke against God
and against Moses. "Why have you brought us up out of
Egypt to die in the wilderness? For there is no food and
no water and we detest this miserable food."*

Numbers 21:4–5

Reflection

Are we there yet? When do we get there?
"The people became impatient on the way."
I am comforted these words are in scripture.
The spiritual life is a journey.
It's human nature to get impatient on the way,
no matter how many miracles already seen.

I lose patience in myself, lose patience with God,
So don't be surprised when I lose patience with you.
I don't want to travel to happiness.
I want to arrive.
I didn't sign up for miserable food, I signed up for a banquet!
Can you blame me for complaining?
Life is short I don't have the time for this!

Patience is the mercy that allows dreams
To climb over failure and disappointment.
Patience makes determination possible.

Patience enables us to ask forgiveness and grant forgiveness
to others.
Patience enables us accept forgiveness and forgive ourselves.
Patience enables us to enjoy our journey
Even when we do not know where we are going or when we will
get there.
Patience is not settling for less or giving up.
Patience is God's gift, giving you time and room to grow.
Fasting for forty days is easy,
Walking the journey of our life with patience is hard.
Love is patient.

Fifth Week in Lent—Wednesday

"If you do not worship the golden statue I have made, you shall immediately be thrown into the furnace of blazing fire, and who is the god that will deliver you out of my hands?" Shadrach, Meshach, and Abednego answered the king, "O Nebuchadnezzar, we have no need to present a defense in this matter. If our God whom we serve is able to deliver us from the furnace of blazing fire and out of your hand, O king, let him deliver us. But if not, be it known to you, O king, that we will not serve your gods and we will not worship the golden statue that you have set up."

Daniel 3:15b–18

Reflection

"Have you prepared your conversation?"
asked the priest sitting across from me my first week in the
    rectory.
He looked like an owl with blue eyes and wavy silver hair.
"Have you prepared your dinner conversation?" he asked again
In his clipped aristocratic New England accent.
I thought he was kidding, more hazing for the baby priest.
He was not kidding.
Fr. Walter J. Sullivan, CSP, was a published Shakespearean
    scholar,
And was not about to waste time on my babble.
When in conversation, as he quoted a line from Shakespeare,
if I could not identify the Act and Scene, much less the play,

the next morning leaning against my door,
would be a brand-new paperback edition of the play,
Certainly, a topic for a future dinner.
It was like living with the headmaster!

Don't get me wrong, he was a gentleman,
and when it was preached at his funeral
"I don't think in his life Walter ever scolded anybody,"
It was the truth.

One conversation surprised me.
He was reminiscing about his years as a chaplain during World
    War II.
From 1942–46 he served as a chaplain to the 379th Bomber
    squadron
Stationed in England at Kimbolton airfield. He talked about
    "the boys."
He celebrated Mass, heard confessions, and before a mission
Blessed each one, Catholic or no, as they climbed into a
    B-17 bomber.
He talked about searching the skies waiting for planes to return,
And for the planes that would never return.
In one short stretch, eighty planes—each with a crew of ten, were
    shot down.
Fr. Walter was blessing men climbing into planes, both priest and
    airmen knowing they may not come back.

He celebrated a Mass for the dead for each soldier, Catholic or no,
He personally wrote a letter to each family
Writing of their boy's bravery and kindness.
As Walter spoke, the pain of writing those letters,
Of blessing those boys, that pain continued to live in his eyes.

Fr. Sullivan's memories make real to me this scripture:

"If our God whom we serve is able to deliver us from the furnace
of blazing fire and out of your hand, O king, let him deliver
us. But if not, be it known to you, O king, that we will not
serve your gods."

The trust it takes to pray to a God who may not deliver you out of
evil hands,

may not deliver you from whatever fiery furnace faces you,

but you are going to live as you believe anyway, that's faith.

I often pray for success—and safety, that's okay.

I need to pray for the courage to live what I believe, whatever
happens.

Fifth Week in Lent—Thursday

When Abram was ninety-nine years old, the LORD appeared to Abram, and said to him, "I am God Almighty, walk with me, and be blameless, and I will make my covenant between me and you, and I will make you exceedingly numerous." Then Abram fell on his face; and God said to him: "As for me, this is my covenant with you: You shall be the ancestor of a multitude of nations. No longer shall your name be called Abram, but your name shall be Abraham; for I have made you the ancestor of a multitude of nations....I will establish my covenant between me and you, and your offspring after you...To be God to you and your offspring after you."

Genesis 17:1–5, 7

Reflection

Rabbis say the difference between Abram and the rest of us is
Abram did not believe in God, Abram believed God.
God not as an idea, whose existence I have concluded is real,
But God who is responsible for my existence,
And gives direction to my life.

Ninety-nine years of being good old Abram, then
Abram believes God and became Abraham—
Someone he didn't know—never dreamed of being.
Ninety-nine years of creating nothing—nothing of value to leave
    behind.
Abraham believes God and as a result
would create enough for a multitude of generations to remember.

God made a promise not only to Abraham—but to all who
    came after
—sight unseen—which is where we come in, descendants of
    Abraham—
Rather than be god, we would believe God.
We tend to think God's interactions with human beings began
    with us
—in truth we are part of a long procession dating beyond Abram,
to whenever it was God decided there should be light,
at least fourteen billion years of cosmic history before Abram's
    ancestors appeared.
It's a long line we stand in, inheritors of divine experience
Written into our DNA and history, both sins and graces.
Now it is our turn, our translation of grace, our experience, our
    faithfulness.
It is not just about us, the line of human experience doesn't end
    with us,
We have an obligation to those who come after us,
The generations for whom we are the saints
Who make it easier or harder for them to believe
That God is God, and they are God's people,
Precious in God's eyes.

Fifth Week in Lent—Friday

All my close friends are watching for me to stumble.
"Perhaps he can be enticed and then we can prevail against him
*   and take our revenge against him."…O LORD of hosts, let me*
*   see your retribution upon them.*

Jeremiah 20:10b, 12

Reflection

Can you imagine Jeremiah's reaction if God forgave his
    "close friends"?
Like Jeremiah we pray for retribution, not reclamation,
The death penalty, not rehabilitation.
We can understand the rationale for those rejecting Jesus
Who made the Samaritan hero to the man who fell in
    with robbers,
Who took the side of the prodigal son against his brother,
Who forgave the woman caught red-handed in adultery,
Who befriended the turncoat tax collector for the Romans,
Who healed the servant of an occupying Roman centurion.
The friend of my enemy is my enemy.
We can understand why some wanted Jesus dead.

Mercy is a mystery; it bites the betrayed and the merciful.
Great minds, zealous souls have struggled for centuries to do so.
One of the greatest minds makes matters worse.
Thomas Aquinas said God even loves the souls in hell!
What is up with that? The souls are in hell only because
They refuse to empty their arms to receive God's embrace.

God still loves them, souls in hell!
Jeremiah makes more sense than Jesus or Thomas Aquinas.

Our world is full of people who have not emptied their arms
to receive God's embrace. Their arms are full of all the
    deadly sins:
pride, greed, lust, envy, gluttony, wrath, sloth.
In their arms they carry the suffering victims of their sins.
To the degree we can protect the victims of their sin,
To the degree we can prevent innocent suffering, we do so.

Since the judgment of the guilty belongs to God alone
I am left to wonder what my arms carry, and how free are they
to accept the embrace of God?

Fifth Week in Lent—Saturday

The chief priests and Pharisees called a meeting of the council, and said, "What are we to do? This man is performing many signs. If we let him go on like this, everyone will believe in him, and the Romans will come, and destroy both our holy place and our nation." But one of them, Caiaphas, who was high priest that year said to them, "You know nothing at all! You do not understand that it is better for one man to die for the people than to have the whole nation destroyed!" So from that day on, they planned to put him to death.

John 11:47–50, 53

Reflection

Collateral damage is part of our decision-making process.
Economic, political, military, religious decisions have
    collateral damage.
Greed creating the subprime mortgage crisis—left collateral
    damage.
Putin's invasion of the Ukraine left collateral damage.
Cutting jobs to meet investor expectations leaves collateral
    damage.
Global warming is the collateral damage of a thousand decisions.
Political decisions almost always involve collateral damage.
Personal decisions, who we love, who we don't,
who we help, who we don't, leave collateral damage.
Most of us have been the collateral damage of someone
    else's decision.

Most of us have created collateral damage by our choices.
The death of Jesus was about collateral damage, not truth,
To those who planned to put him to death,
Which, at the very least should give me pause, and consider
The collateral damage left behind in the wake of my decisions.
All too easily the truth and the One who is the Truth
Can be the collateral damage of what I do and fail to do.

Palm Sunday—Year A

*A very large crowd spread their cloaks on the road, and others cut
branches from trees and spread them on the road. The crowds
that went ahead of him and that followed were shouting,
"Hosanna to the Son of David! Blessed is he who comes in the
name of the Lord! Hosannah in the highest!"*

Matthew 21:8–9

*From noon on, darkness came over the whole land until three in the
afternoon. And about three o'clock Jesus cried with a loud voice,
"Eli Eli, lema sabachthani? That is, "My God, my God, why
have you forsaken me?"*

Matthew 27:46

Reflection

So many things begin well and end badly,
Which is the story of Palm Sunday.
I think, perhaps you do as well, when things are going well,
I am being blessed.
When for me things go badly (or are even blandly),
God is more obscure, less generous, less present,
I am not as favored as I was when things were going well.
It may be my fault, it may be God's fault, but there it is.

Jesus was blessed, favored by God, on Palm Sunday.
Jesus was blessed, favored by God, on Good Friday.
We, of course, did not know that till Easter Sunday,

But God was present to Jesus in the Palm Sunday triumph
And if anything, even closer to him on Good Friday.

On the cross, it may not have felt that way to Jesus,
"My God, my God, why have you forsaken me"
Even if the opening verse of a psalm, meant something after all.
To follow Jesus on Palm Sunday, is to remember:
God is with you in good times and in bad.
How I feel, no matter how badly I feel, Is not an accurate
    measure of
how I am loved or how valuable I am—to God.

Priest and psychologist, I have seen hard times, lonely times,
Times of rejection, times of suffering that make any human being
feel worthless, hopeless. Their lives robbed of any goodness.
How much you are loved, how valuable you are,
Is not measured by the pain you feel,
It is measured only by the crucified Lord.
Jesus crucified is the measure of how much you are loved
    by God.
That is hard to feel, but it is true, which makes it worth believing.

Palm Sunday is followed by the pain of Good Friday,
Which is followed by the wild, fantastic Resurrection of
    Easter Sunday,
Which is followed by our life everlasting, loved by God, world
    without end.

Palm Sunday—Year B

*He took with him Peter, James, and John, and began to be distressed
and agitated, and said to them, "I am deeply grieved, even to
death; remain here, keep awake."...He came and found them
sleeping.*

Mark 14:33–34, 37

*All of them deserted him and fled. A certain young man was
following him, wearing nothing but a linen cloth. They caught
hold of him, but he left the linen cloth and ran off naked.*

Mark 14:50–52

*At three o'clock Jesus cried out with a loud voice, "Eloi, Eloi, lema
sabachthani?" which means, "My God, my God, why have you
forsaken me?"*

Mark 15:34

Reflection

Loneliness left no marks in his hands or feet,
So, there is no devotion to Jesus the Lonely.
But loneliness was a suffering he carried.
Jesus was anxious, asking friends to be with him.
In the garden he threw himself down on the ground
begging, weeping, pleading, crying,
that this pain would not happen to him.
His friends did not hear him—they were sleeping.

Friends with whom he ate dinner,
Friends who promised to be with him,
Ran away naked just to get away from him,
Leaving him to face his fate alone.

Jesus dies alone.
In Mark's Gospel there are no consoling figures
at the foot the cross to share his pain.
He suffers alone.
Loneliness so severe that even Jesus
feels abandoned by the God he always trusted.
Jesus was alone.

Loneliness leaves no marks on our hands or feet either.
It is not obvious to others when we are lonely
And when we are, we have learned to hide it.
Paradoxically, loneliness does not draw people toward us;
It pushes them away—
People running away naked into the night
That they are not overwhelmed by our pain.

Loneliness is a fact of modern life,
the collateral damage of progress.
People move, no choice
but to follow jobs to survive,
to succeed.
Families, neighbors, are memories—
special occasions—not everyday life.
The pressures of life making strangers
of those who share the same bed—how alone is that?
We don't even pray together anymore
The lonely denied even that Sunday comfort.
You are hardly ever too young to be lonely—
People rail against the evils of social media,

But what if TikTok is your only friend?
The old expect to be lonely, the best to be hoped for—
The occasional kindness of strangers.
We die alone, far from home, far from friends.

The truth is that many more than we know
or would ever like to know
suffer their pains, their tortures, alone.
Jesus suffers alone because they suffer alone.
Jesus hangs on the cross because we hang on our own cross,
and Jesus, who knows what it is to suffer alone,
will not leave us in pain by ourselves;
he is there, sharing our lonely cross.

Palm Sunday—Year C

One of the criminals who were hanged there kept derid-
ing him and saying, "Are you not the Messiah? Save your-
self and us!" But the other rebuked him, saying, "Do you
not fear God, since you are under the same sentence of
condemnation? And we indeed have been condemned
justly, for we are getting what we deserve for our deeds,
but this man has done nothing wrong." Then he said,
"Jesus, remember me when you come into your kingdom."
He replied, "Truly I tell you, today you will be with me
in Paradise."

Luke 23:39–43

Reflection

Remember me:
Says the man who has been forgotten.
Remember me:
Says the man who is in no way memorable.
Remember me:
Says the man we really do not remember.
Remember me:
And all we remember is that he confessed
to being a man whose crimes deserved crucifixion, a torture of
    asphyxiation,
We do remember that.
We remember he used his last breaths to defend Jesus.
We remember that in the entire crucifixion he is the only one to
    defend Jesus.

The last words, the last kind words—the last believing words—
    Jesus heard
Belonged to a man whose name nobody remembers.
"Remember me when you come into your kingdom."
We remember these words as we begin Holy Week,
a week devoted to remembering Jesus, that when the time comes,
when our breaths are numbered, Jesus will remember us into
    Paradise.

Holy Week—Monday

*They gave a dinner for him. Martha serves, and Lazarus
was one of those at the table with him. Mary took a pound
of costly perfume made of pure nard, anointed Jesus' feet,
and wiped them with her hair. The house was filled with
the fragrance of her perfume.*

John 12:2–3

Reflection

Mary and Jesus were friends.
Bethany was a safe place
filled with the fragrance of perfumed oil Mary massaged into
    his feet
With extravagant care.

"Life is measured by love," Pope Francis observes.
In a week promising to be among the saddest
Now is the time for gestures of extravagant love.
What are we saving ourselves for—if not extravagant love?
This is the second time the Gospels report Jesus's feet as the
    object of caress:
An unknown sinner woman washed them with her tears,
And Mary of Bethany's fragrant massage.
These women made an impression on Jesus, who,
when it is time to show care for his friends,
to make clear the meaning of his life, washes their feet.
Jesus learned from these women, so can we.

As Pope Francis preaches:
"May we reach out to those who are suffering and those most
    in need.
May we not be concerned about what we lack,
but what good we can do for others."[10] Amen.

10. Pope Francis, Homily for Palm Sunday, April 6, 2020, https://slmedia.org/blog/pope
-francis-homily-for-palm-sunday-2.

Holy Week—Tuesday

Jesus was troubled in spirit, and declared, "Very truly, I tell you, one of you will betray me." The disciples looked at one another, uncertain of whom he was speaking. One of his disciples—the one whom Jesus loved—was reclining next to him; Simon Peter therefore motioned to him to ask Jesus of whom he was speaking. So, while reclining next to Jesus, he asked him, "Lord, who is it?" Jesus answered, "It is the one to whom I give this piece of bread when I have dipped it in the dish." So when he had dipped the piece of bread, he gave it to Judas son of Simon Iscariot. After he received the piece of bread, Satan entered into him. Jesus said to him, "Do quickly what you are going to do." Now, no one at table knew why he said this to him....

Peter said to him, "Lord why cannot I follow you now? I will lay down my life for you." Jesus answered, "Will you lay down your life for me? Very truly I tell you, before the cock crows, you will have denied me three times."

John 13:21–28, 37–38

Reflection

There are lots of stories I tell about myself.
I tell stories about my failures, my struggles, my doubts.
I tell stories of being afraid, sad, lost.
I never tell stories about my betrayals.
It isn't that they are not there—I have plenty,

All too available to my memory, dripping with shame.
I don't easily, actually ever, share these stories.
But Jesus knows them all.
He knew about Judas. He knew about Peter.
He knew all of them would leave him alone.
Still, he had supper, his last supper, with them.
He washed their feet and promised he would be with them,
Knowing they would all betray him before morning.
So, when people feel that they don't deserve the Eucharist,
When people decide they don't deserve to be forgiven,
And particularly, when people point out others who should
    be denied
Table fellowship—Eucharist—communion— with Jesus,
They are not paying attention.
Jesus's last supper with his disciples and every supper after that—
Two thousand years of eating and drinking in his memory,
Are meals Jesus chooses to eat with sinners—with people who
    make mistakes, with those who have, and will again, betray
    a promise.

The Eucharist, communion, is all about Jesus, not about me.
It isn't that betrayals don't matter,
it is because they do matter that Jesus invites me, and Judas,
Peter and all the others, to eat and drink with him,
to draw strength from his forgiveness and love.

If it is safe for you, if it is possible for you, I encourage you,
This Easter season, to break bread with the Risen Lord.
I don't care how long it has been since you have been to church
It isn't about you; it's about him.
It's about letting yourself be loved by him,
Which is all he ever wants to do.

Holy Week—Wednesday

The Lord has given me a well-trained tongue that I may know how to sustain the weary with a word. Morning by morning he wakens—wakens my ear to listen as those who are taught. The Lord has opened my ear, and I was not rebellious, I did not turn backward. I gave my cheeks to those who pulled out the beard; I did not hide my face from insult and spitting. The Lord God helps me; therefore, I have not been disgraced; therefore, I have set my face like flint, and I know I shall not be put to shame; he who vindicates me is near. Who will contend with me? Let us stand together. Who are my adversaries? Let them confront me.

Isaiah 50:4–8

Reflection

To speak a word that will rouse the weary, seems pretty
    small stuff
for the serious reflections of Holy Week.
Then again, there is a shortage of reassuring words out there.
Days are filled with meaningless hellos, gruff orders, persistent
    criticism.
People throw shame like snowballs—aiming for our heads.
We are sworn at, even threatened.
Heads seldom rest on pillows plumped with encouragement.

My tongue is trained to notice distinctions, divisions,
Nuance, inconsistencies, error, annoyance,

And share them with vigor.
Would it be so hard to shut up?
Would it be so hard to replace all that with words, any words,
any gentle recognition that someone is struggling,
Frayed, weary, tired from trying, perhaps
worn down and worn out by advice,
continual reminders someone else does it
whatever it is, better and faster?

How well trained does a tongue have to be to be kind?
A little bit goes a long way, can make our day.
These words, simple and few as they are
Take the sting out of the day.
A few words only—enough to make our heart jump out of bed
And continue our journey.

It seems penny-ante, cheap spiritual advice, until I started
     thinking
in my mind's eye. From the moment Jesus was arrested—
All he heard was screaming, cackling, insulting, jeering.
Words of insult, disbelief, and humiliation.
All those sneering self-satisfied words driving into his brain
Long before a nail was ever driven into his flesh.
A few words to sustain the weary doesn't seem so paltry after all.
I worry: what words my well-trained tongue has been speaking
     all Lent long?

Holy Thursday

And during supper Jesus, knowing that the Father had given all things into his hands, and that he had come from God and was going to God, got up from the table, took off his outer robe, and tied a towel around himself. Then he poured water into a basin and began to wash the disciples' feet and to wipe them with the towel that was tied around him.

John 13:3–5

Reflection

When a baby is born
Every part of that child is cuddled and kissed.
Parents, especially grandparents
Nanas, Grandpas, Omas & Opas, Abuelas y Abuelos
cannot resist kissing and sucking its fingers and toes.
It is how we communicate to someone who cannot understand us
that our love for them is unconditional.
But time marches on, our personalities develop,
And we disappoint and are disappointed.
Our feet grow—less attractive,
Larger, sweatier, some of us hairier,
Decorated by calluses and scars, purpled by varicose veins
Aching, arthritic; they become symbols
Of those aspects of ourselves we hide from others.
Few people seek to suck on our fingers and toes now—
Except Jesus.
Jesus who sees us so clearly,

Who knows better than we know, our broken parts,
Who knows in us, as he knew in his disciples,
Just where our breaking point is.
Jesus, who knows just what conditions,
Just what fears, just what appetites will lead us to betray
those we swear we love,
Jesus, knowing all of this, washes the feet of his disciples.

He wants touch to burn memory in their brain,
The memory of his flesh touching theirs.
When their feet run away from him as fast as they can,
Jesus wants them to recall he held those feet in his hands
Caressed them, kissed them, wiped them dry
Because he loved them.
Because he loved them, they were to love one another.

They did not understand the Last Supper.
They would not understand Good Friday.
They would not be waiting for Easter Sunday.
They would remember, when the smoke cleared,
that Jesus washed their feet, and his touch, that particular mercy
is all the theology they needed to explain
the Last Supper, Good Friday, and Easter Sunday.

Every Eucharist we celebrate is the risen Lord touching our flesh.
Every Good Friday is the memory of his love.
Every Easter Sunday, the risen Lord rinses the sin and sweat
Off our feet, off our souls.

Every time we gather, we promise to do as he did.
Never mind that we fail; every Eucharist washes us clean,
Wraps a towel around our waist, and sets us off, water in hand,
To wash feet in his name, in his Spirit.

Good Friday

*They took Jesus; and carrying the cross by himself, he
went out to what is called The Place of the Skull, which
in Hebrew is called Golgotha. There they crucified him,
and with him two others, one on either side, with Jesus
between them....When Jesus knew that all was now finished, he said (in order to fulfill the scripture), "I am
thirsty." A jar full of sour wine was standing there. They
put a sponge full of the wine on a branch of hyssop and
held it to his mouth.*

*When Jesus had received the wine, he said, "It is
finished." Then he bowed his head and gave up his spirit.*

John 19:16b–18, 28–30

Reflection

To crucify a man you strip him naked,
stretch his arms wide on a wooden beam,
Carefully locate the space between two bones
just below his wrist and drive the nail through, securing the arm
    to a beam.
A rope pulls the beam up high enough
so that the victim's feet cannot touch the ground.
Then you take the kicking feet and secure them to either side of
    the post
Driving a nail through one and the other.
Then you step back and watch the torture begin.

His full weight hanging on the spikes
the man in the mutilated body realizes he cannot breathe.
He has to flex the muscles in his arms and chest
And pull himself up against the nails in his wrist
(Like a gymnast doing an iron cross on the rings)
And then gasp for air until the pain in his wrists is too great
or his muscles give out. When he feels this about to happen
he gradually slides his body down the cross
Pushing his weight on the nails in his feet.
When the pain in his feet is too much to handle or he runs short
    of breath,
he flexes the muscles in his chest and arms
And using the nails between his bones as leverage,
Once more pulls himself up so he can gasp for air.
The crucified will repeat this process
Over and over again; forced to inflict on himself one pain
in order to buy relief from the other excruciating pain.
No matter what he does he is never pain-free,
Something always hurts.
Some crucified grow delirious,
all grow tired.
Gradually losing the ability
To pull themselves up for the precious air
That sustains their suffering life,
The crucified realize that sooner rather than later
They will have to just let their body
Hang, until they breathe their last.

When we see a crucifixion represented in art
We see a body hanging passively from the cross.
Crucifixion was not a passive punishment.
Crucifixion forced the man to torture himself
Until he realized that he had no choice
But to be his own executioner and let himself die.

In John's Gospel, Jesus looks evil right in the face
And dares it to do the worst it can do
And that is how he came to be crucified:
Pulling himself up and down the cross
Fighting for each breath
Until he decides that it is finished
And bowing his head, hands his Spirit back to his Father.
Why does Jesus choose this?
How does this, as we say, "save us?'
What is there to celebrate in a tragedy where once again
Evil kills another good man?

We know no one stole Jesus's life from him.
He gave it because his Father wanted all people to know
that his love, God's love, for us has no limits:
"for God so loved the world that he gave his only begotten Son.
Jesus did not come into the world to condemn the world
but to save it" (John 3:16). That includes Judas, and you, and me,
     and all those other people, then and now who continue to put
     Jesus to death.

But today is not about what we have done.
It is not about our faults, our failings, our sins.
Today is about what Jesus has already done for those of us,
Who continue to crucify God among men, women, and children.
Jesus chooses the cross showing us the Love who is God
Searches out men, women, and children wherever they are
     suffering
and embraces them.
Jesus chooses the cross to tell us that he is not afraid of evil.
Jesus chooses the cross to tell us that he is not afraid of us.

Jesus is waiting for us to climb through our faults and failures;
Jesus is waiting for us to climb through tears, grief, and doubt;

Jesus is waiting for us to climb the ladder of our faith,
     whatever it is,
Have dinner with him and be his disciple.

Jesus is waiting, to accompany you on your journey.
How long you take to get there and join him, now that is
     up to you.